HAL LEONARD
GUITAR METHOD

COMPLETE EDITION

Contains books 1, 2, and 3 bound together in one easy-to-use volume

BY WILL SCHMID
AND GREG KOCH

O9-ABI-969

Speed • Pitch • Balance • Loop

To access audio visit:
www.halleonard.com/mylibrary

Enter Code
3912-3953-3215-7369

ISBN 978-0-634-04701-5

7777 W. BLUEMOUND RD. P.O. BOX 13819 MILWAUKEE, WI 53213

Visit Hal Leonard Online at
www.halleonard.com

YOUR GUITAR

This book is designed for use with any type of guitar—acoustic steel-string, nylon-string classical, or electric. Any of these guitars can be adapted for use in a wide variety of styles of music.

STEEL-STRING

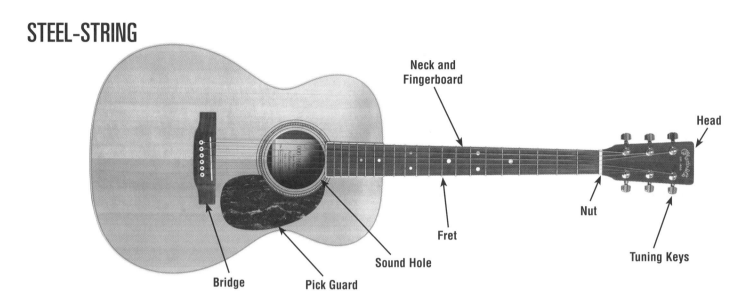

NYLON-STRING

ELECTRIC

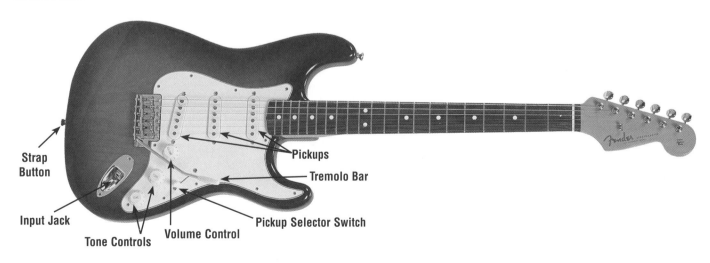

If you are using a solidbody-electric or an acoustic-electric be sure to practice with an amplifier some of the time.

TUNING

TUNING TO THE AUDIO

When you are tuning your guitar, you will adjust the pitch (highness or lowness of sound) of each string by turning the corresponding tuning key. Tightening a string raises the pitch and loosening it lowers the pitch.

The strings are numbered 1 through 6 beginning with the thinnest string, the one closest to your knee. Tune each string in sequence beginning with the first string, by listening to the correct pitch on the audio and slowly turning the tuning key until the sound of the string matches the sound on the track.

TUNING WITH AN ELECTRONIC TUNER

An electronic tuner "reads" the pitch of a sound and tells you whether or not the pitch is correct. Until your ear is well trained in hearing pitches, this can be a much more accurate way to tune. There are many different types of tuners available, and each one will come with more detailed instructions for its use.

TUNING TO A KEYBOARD

If you have a piano or electric keyboard nearby, play the correct key (see diagram) and slowly turn the corresponding tuning key until the sound of the string matches the sound of the keyboard.

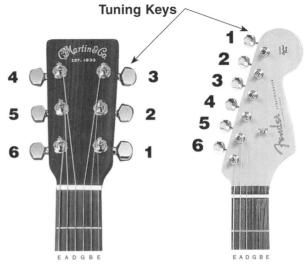

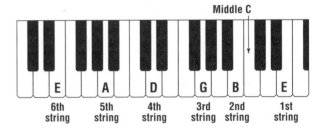

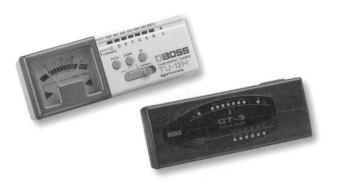

ANOTHER WAY TO TUNE

To check or correct your tuning when no pitch source is available, follow these steps:
- Assume that the sixth string is tuned correctly to E.
- Press the sixth string at the 5th fret. This is the pitch A to which you tune your open fifth string. Play the depressed sixth string and the fifth string with your thumb. When the two sounds match, you are in tune.
- Press the fifth string at the 5th fret and tune the open fourth string to it. Follow the same procedure that you did on the fifth and sixth strings.
- Press the fourth string at the 5th fret and tune the open third string to it.
- To tune the second string, press the third string at the 4th fret and tune the open second string to it.
- Press the second string at the 5th fret and tune the first string to it.

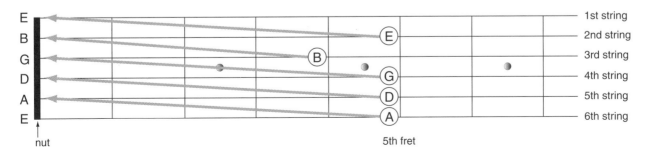

This is called **relative tuning** because the strings are tuned relative to one another.

PLAYING POSITION

There are several ways to hold the guitar comfortably. On the left is a typical seated position, and on the right is the standing position. Make sure you practice sitting and standing. Observe the following general guidelines in forming your playing posture:

- Position your body, arms, and legs in such a way that you avoid tension.

- If you feel tension creeping into your playing, you probably need to reassess your position.

- Tilt the neck upwards—never down.

- Keep the body of the guitar as vertical as possible. Avoid slanting the top of the guitar so that you can see better. Balance your weight evenly from left to right. Sit straight (but not rigid).

Left-hand fingers are numbered 1 through 4 (Pianists: Note that the thumb is not number 1.) Place the thumb in back of the neck roughly opposite the 2nd finger. Avoid gripping the neck like a baseball bat with the palm touching the back of the neck.

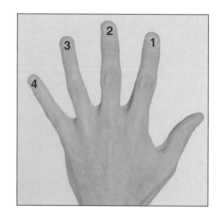

These photos show the position for holding a pick and the right-hand position in relationship to the strings. Strive for finger efficiency and relaxation in your playing.

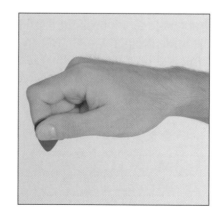

MUSICAL SYMBOLS

Music is written in **notes** on a **staff**. The staff has five lines and four spaces between the lines. Where a note is written on the staff determines its **pitch** (highness or lowness). At the beginning of the staff is a **clef sign**. Guitar music is written in the treble clef.

STAFF   **TREBLE CLEF**

Each line and space of the staff has a letter name. The **lines** are, (from bottom to top) E - G - B - D - F, which you can remember as Every Guitarist Begins Doing Fine. The **spaces** are, (from bottom to top) F - A - C - E, which spells "Face."

LINES   E   G   B   D   F   **SPACES**   F   A   C   E

The staff is divided into several parts by bar lines. The space between two bar lines is called a **measure** (also known as a "bar"). To end a piece of music a double bar is placed on the staff.

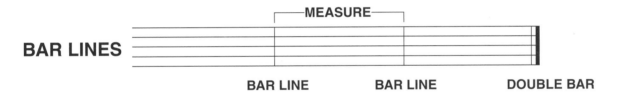

BAR LINES   MEASURE

BAR LINE   BAR LINE   DOUBLE BAR

Each measure contains a group of **beats**. Beats are the steady pulse of music. You respond to the pulse or beat when you tap your foot.

The two numbers placed next to the clef sign are the time signature.
The top number tells you how many beats are in one measure.

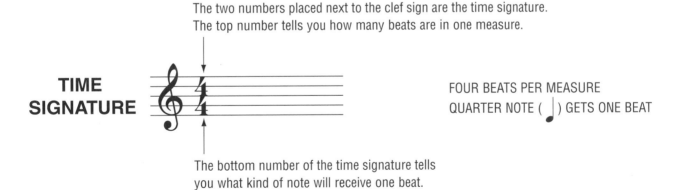

TIME SIGNATURE   FOUR BEATS PER MEASURE
QUARTER NOTE (♩) GETS ONE BEAT

The bottom number of the time signature tells you what kind of note will receive one beat.

Notes indicate the length (number of counts) of musical sound.

NOTES   WHOLE NOTE = 4 beats   HALF NOTE = 2 beats   QUARTER NOTE = 1 beat

When different kinds of notes are placed on different lines or spaces, you will know the pitch of the note and how long to play the sound.

NOTES ON THE FIRST STRING

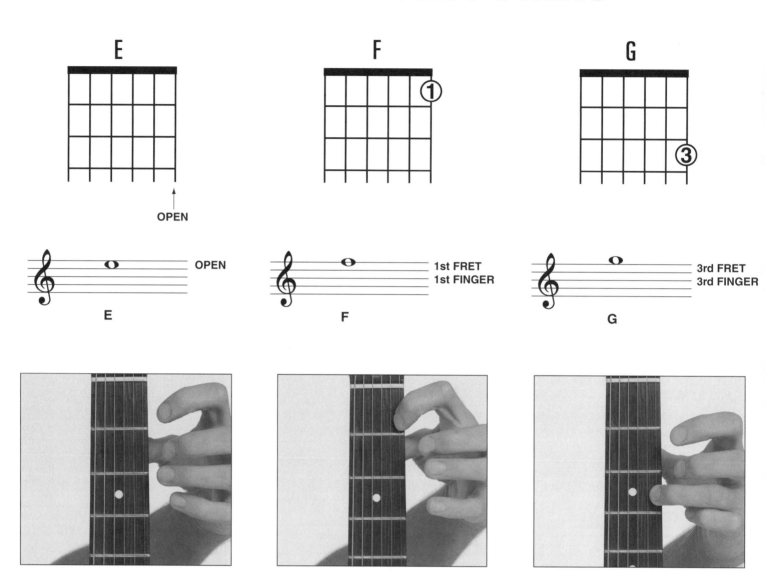

E   F   G

OPEN

E   OPEN
F   1st FRET / 1st FINGER
G   3rd FRET / 3rd FINGER

This sign (⊓) tells you to strike the string with a downward motion of the pick.

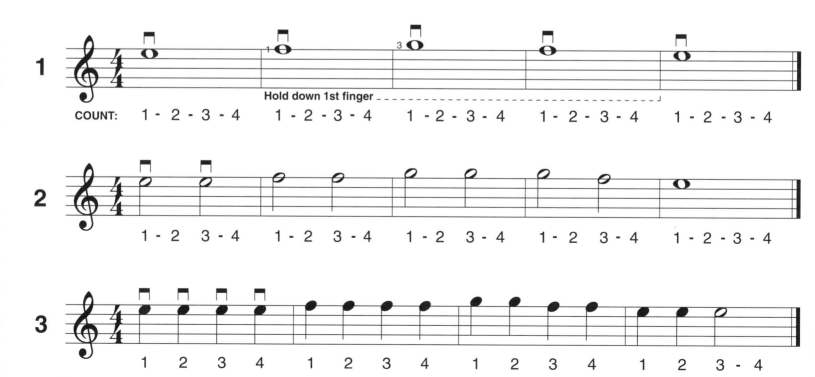

1

COUNT: 1 - 2 - 3 - 4   1 - 2 - 3 - 4   1 - 2 - 3 - 4   1 - 2 - 3 - 4   1 - 2 - 3 - 4

Hold down 1st finger

2

1 - 2   3 - 4   1 - 2   3 - 4   1 - 2   3 - 4   1 - 2   3 - 4   1 - 2 - 3 - 4

3

1   2   3   4   1   2   3   4   1   2   3   4   1   2   3 - 4

At first practice the exercises slowly and steadily. When you can play them well at a slow speed, gradually increase the tempo (speed).

Touch only the tips of the fingers on the strings.

Keep the left hand fingers arched over the strings.

Some songs are longer than one line. When you reach the end of the first line of music, continue on to the second line without stopping. Gray letters above the staff indicate chords to be played by your teacher. Measure numbers are given at the beginning of each new line of music.

Listen to one measure of clicks on the track before playing.

SPANISH THEME

NOTES ON THE SECOND STRING

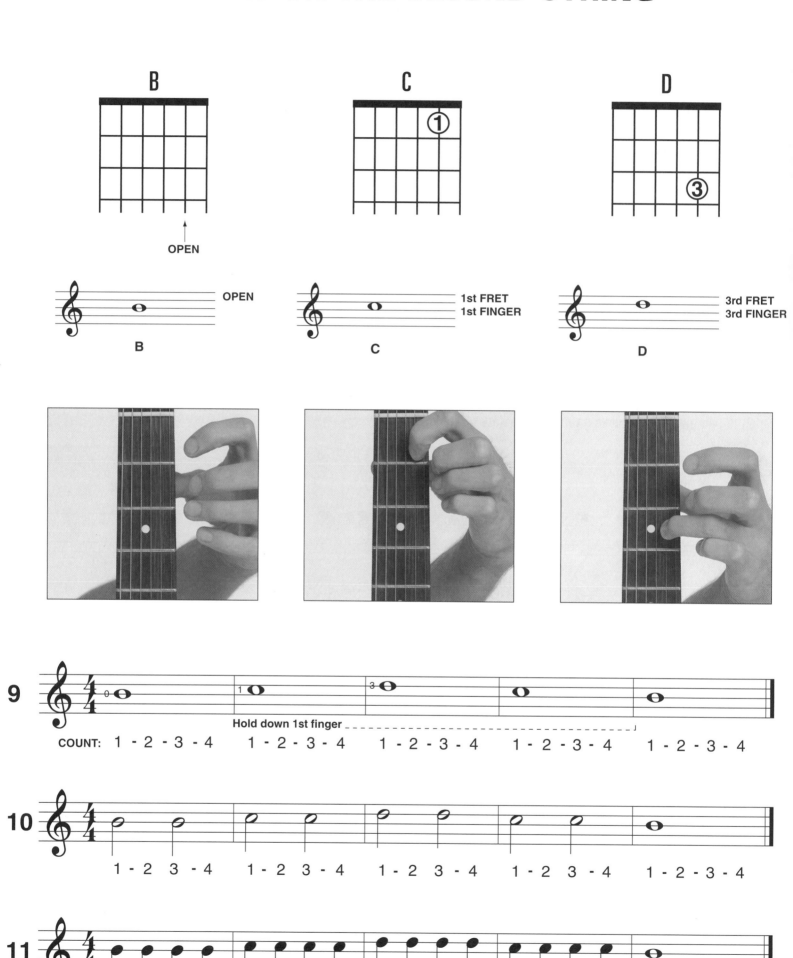

10

Always practice the exercises slowly and steadily at first. After you can play them well at a slower tempo, gradually increase the speed. If some of your notes are fuzzy or unclear, move your left-hand finger slightly until you get a clear sound.

MOVING FROM STRING TO STRING

You have learned six notes now, three on the first string and three on the second string. In the following exercises you will be moving from string to string. As you are playing one note, look ahead to the next and get your fingers in position.

STRING: ② ①
FINGER: open 1st 3rd open 1st 3rd

WORLD BEAT

Practice these songs played on strings 1 and 2. Always begin slowly and then gradually increase the tempo. Gray chord symbols are used throughout the book to indicate that the chords should be played by the instructor.

Some tracks such as "Ode to Joy" are recorded at both a slow and a faster tempo.

ODE TO JOY

Beethoven

BLUES

NOTES ON THE THIRD STRING

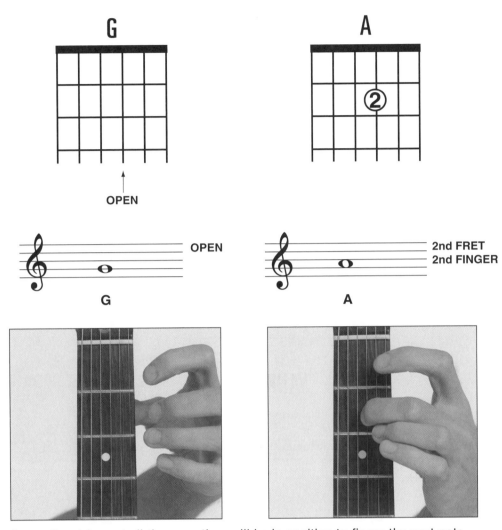

G OPEN

A 2nd FRET / 2nd FINGER

Keep the fingers arched over the strings at all times so they will be in position to finger the next note.

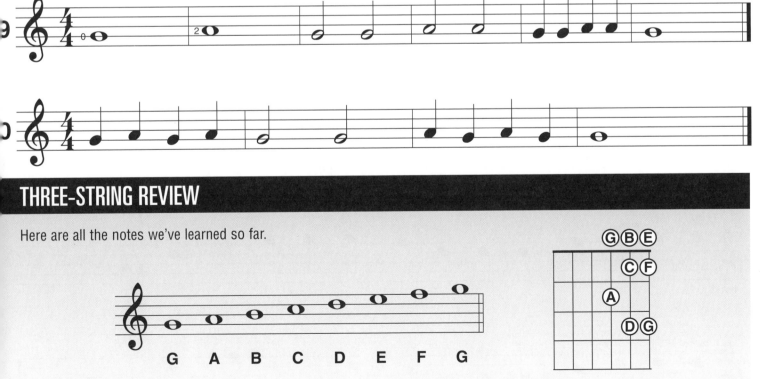

THREE-STRING REVIEW

Here are all the notes we've learned so far.

G A B C D E F G

Play through these notes up and down. Then play just the low G and the high G, and notice how similar they sound. The distance between two different notes with the same letter name is called an **octave**.

The following songs use notes on strings 1, 2, and 3.

ROCKIN' ROBIN

J. Thomas

YANKEE DOODLE

Traditional

SURF ROCK

A **duet** is a song that has two parts that can be played together. Practice both parts of the following duet. Ask your instructor or a friend to play the duet with you, or play either part with the track.

AU CLAIR DE LA LUNE

France

AURA LEE

Poulton/Fosdick

3/4 TIME

Some music has three beats per measure instead of four. This is indicated by the top number of the time signature. The bottom number (4) tells you that the quarter note gets one beat.

A dot after a note increases its value by one-half. In $\frac{3}{4}$ time a dotted half note ( ) gets three beats.

THREE BEATS PER MEASURE
QUARTER NOTE ( ) GETS ONE BEAT

2 beats + 1 beat = 3 beats

COUNT: 1 2 3   1 - 2 3   1 2 3   1 - 2 - 3   1 2 - 3   1 - 2 - 3

HE'S A JOLLY GOOD FELLOW

England

NOTES ON THE FOURTH STRING

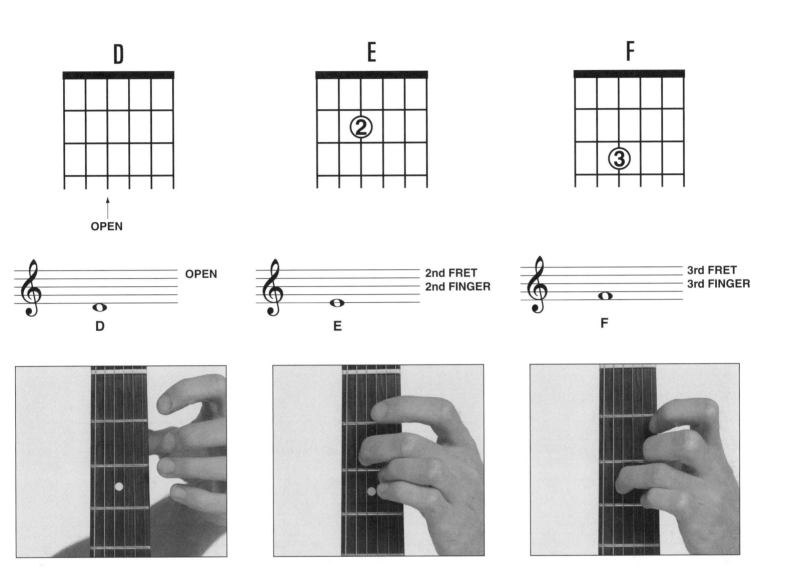

Practice each exercise carefully. Remember to keep your fingers arched over the strings.

PICKUP NOTES

Music doesn't always begin on beat one. When you begin after beat one, the notes before the first full measure are called **pickup notes**. Following are two examples of pickup notes. Count the missing beats out loud before you begin playing.

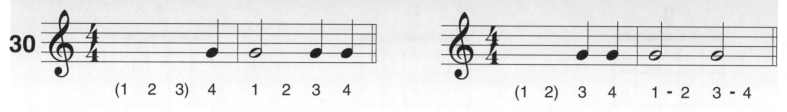

When a song begins with pickup notes, the last measure will be short the exact number of beats used as pickups.

WORRIED MAN BLUES

Traditional

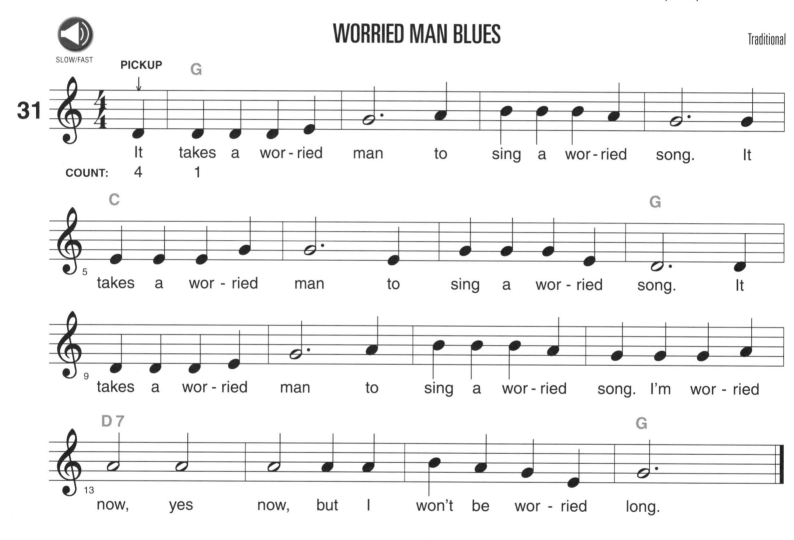

PLAYING CHORDS

A **chord** is sounded when more than two notes or strings are played at the same time. To begin you will be playing chords on three strings with only one finger depressed. Disregard the light gray finger numbers on strings 4, 5, and 6 until you can easily play the one-finger versions of the chords below.

The C Chord
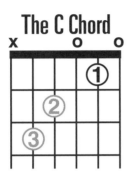

The G7 Chord

Study the illustrations for the chords above. An "o" above a string indicates that the string should be played "open" (not depressed by a finger). An "x" above a string indicates that the string should not be strummed. Refer to the hand positions in the photos below for additional visual guidance.

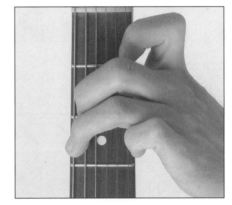

Depress the strings indicated with the tips of your fingers. Arch your fingers to avoid touching strings that are to be played open. Strum over the strings with a downward motion. All strings should sound as one, not separately.

Practice the following exercise strumming once for each slash mark. Keep a steady beat, and change chord fingerings quickly.

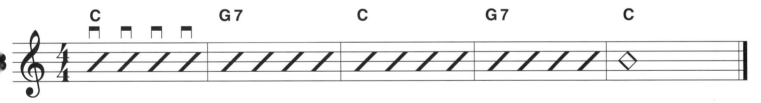

Now apply this strum to the song below.

TOM DOOLEY

Traditional

Next, let's try two more chords: G and D7. Notice that the G chord can be played two different ways.

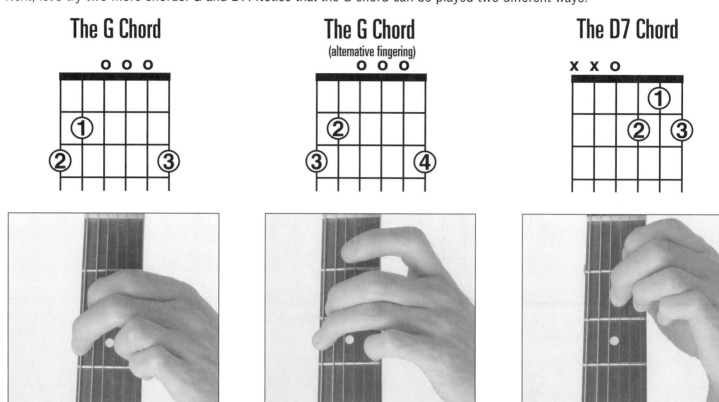

The G Chord

The G Chord
(alternative fingering)

The D7 Chord

Strum once for each slash mark below.

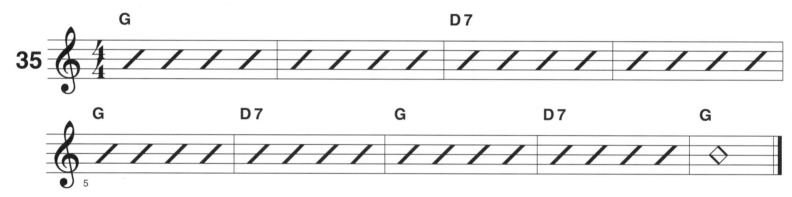

35 G D7

G D7 G D7 G

Review the fingering for the C chord and then practice Exercise 36 until you can play it well. Whenever you are moving between the C chord and the D7 chord, keep the first finger down.

36 G C D7 G

PAY ME MY MONEY DOWN

Georgia Sea Islands

37 G D7

Pay me, oh pay me, pay me my mon - ey down.

G

Pay me or go to jail, pay me my mon - ey down.

The following exercises use the four chords you have learned so far. The chords are arranged in sequences called **chord progressions**.

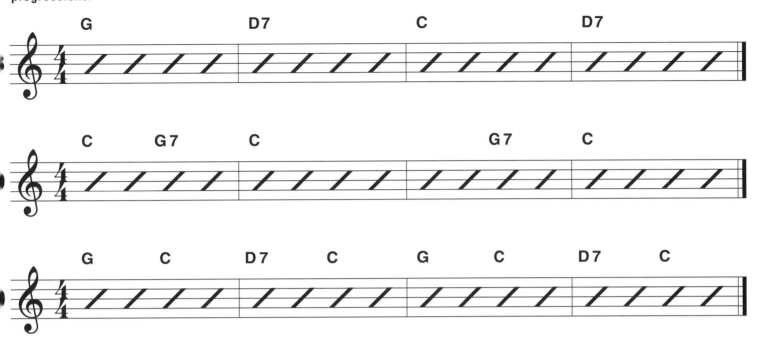

MOVING FROM CHORD TO CHORD

As you are playing one chord, look ahead to the next and get your fingers in position. Then, switch chords using a minimum of hand motion.

Trade off strumming the chords and playing the melody with your teacher or a friend.

12-BAR ROCK

You can also play the G, C, and D7 chords with "Worried Man Blues" on page 16.

TIES

A curved line which connects two notes of the same pitch is called a **tie**. The first note is struck and held for the value of both notes. The second note should not be played again. Look at the following example of tied notes.

42

```
1 - 2 - 3 - 4 - 1     2     3 - 4 - 1 - 2     3     4 - 1     2 - 3 - 4
        5 BEATS                    4 BEATS              2 BEATS
```

Practice trading off on melody and chords in these pieces.

AMAZING GRACE

Traditional

43

A - maz - ing   grace,   how   sweet   the   sound   that

```
                    1 - 2 - 3 - 1 - 2
```

saved   a   wretch   like   me. _____   I   once   was   lost,   but

```
                                        1 - 2 - 3 - 1 - 2
```

now   am   found;   was   blind,   but   now   I   see. _____

RIFFIN'

SLOW/FAST

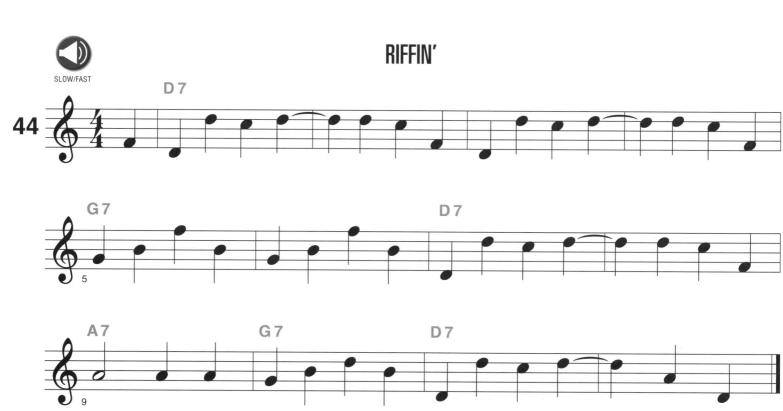

44

22

SLOW/FAST

WHEN THE SAINTS GO MARCHING IN

Traditional

(1) 2   3   4   1-2-3-4-   1   2   3   4   1-2-3-4-   1   2   3   4
Oh when the   saints _____   go march-ing   in _____   oh when the

                              1-2-3-4-1-2   3   4   1-2-3   4
saints   go   march-ing   in _____   Lord, I   want   to

           1   2-3-4-1-2   3   4   1-2-3-4-1
be   in that num-ber _____   when the saints go   march-ing   in. _____

WILL THE CIRCLE BE UNBROKEN

Country Gospel

Will   the   cir - cle _____   be un - bro - ken, _____   by and

by,   Lord,   by   and   by? _____   There's a

bet - ter _____   home a - wait - ing, _____   in   the

sky,   Lord, _____   in   the _____   sky. _____

NOTES ON THE FIFTH STRING

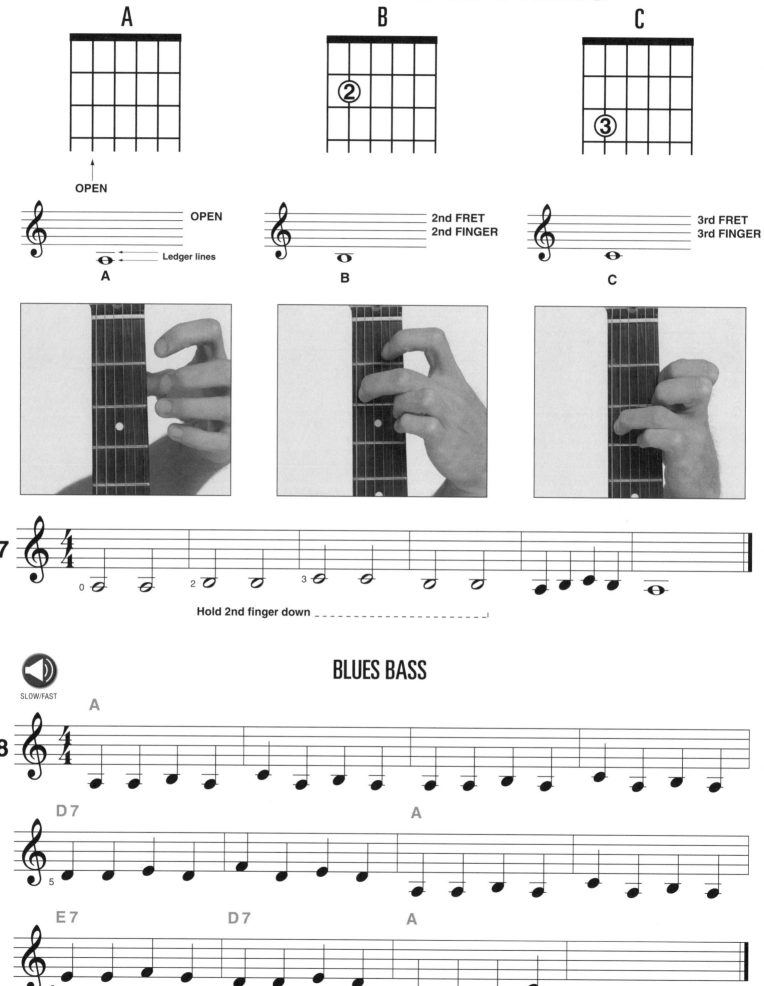

Practice these familiar melodies until you feel comfortable playing them. Remember to look ahead as you play so you can prepare for the next notes.

JOSHUA FOUGHT THE BATTLE OF JERICHO

Spiritual

GREENSLEEVES

England

NOTES ON THE SIXTH STRING

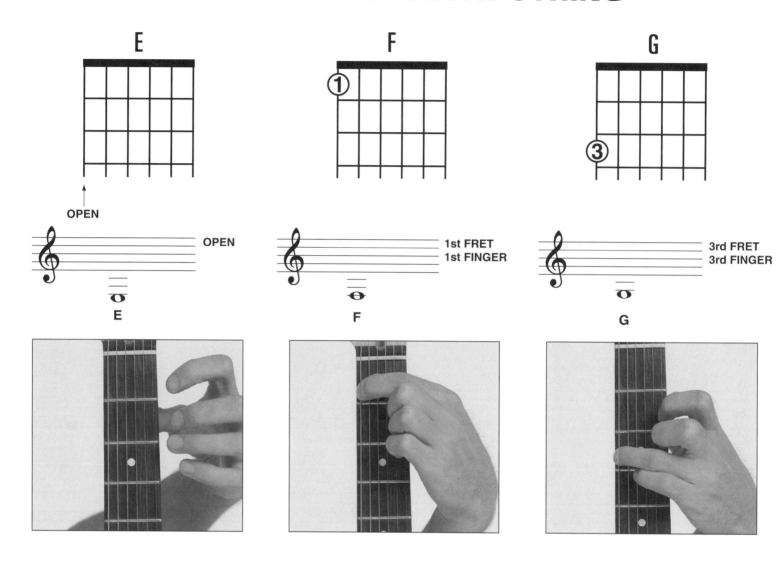

After you play these exercises, write the letter names below each note.

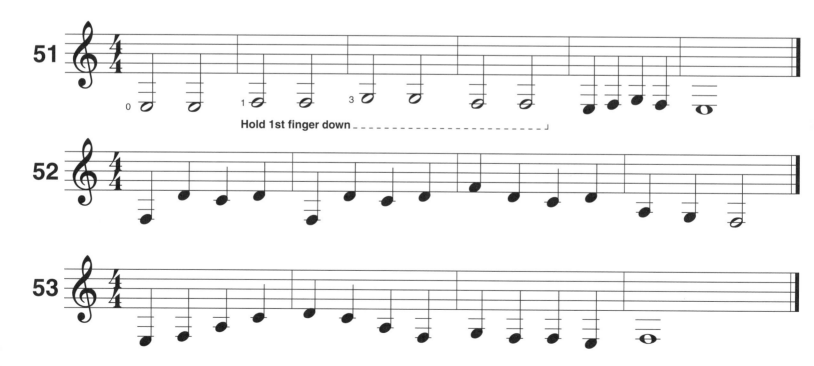

DOO-WOP

GIVE MY REGARDS TO BROADWAY

George M. Cohan

BASS ROCK

HALF AND WHOLE STEPS

The distance between music tones is measured by half steps and whole steps. On your guitar the distance between one fret and the next fret is a half step. The distance from one fret to the third fret in either direction is called a whole step.

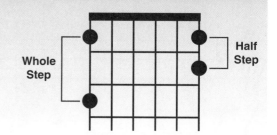

F-SHARP (F♯)

When a **sharp** (♯) is placed in front of a note, the note is raised a half step and played one fret higher. A sharp placed before a note affects all notes on the same line or space that follow in that measure. Following are the three F♯s that appear on the fretboard to the right:

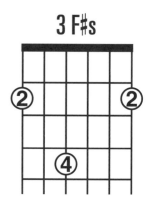

3 F♯s

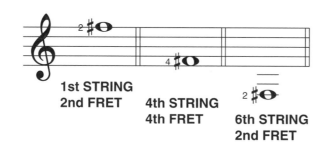

1st STRING
2nd FRET

4th STRING
4th FRET

6th STRING
2nd FRET

Practice each of these finger exercises many times.

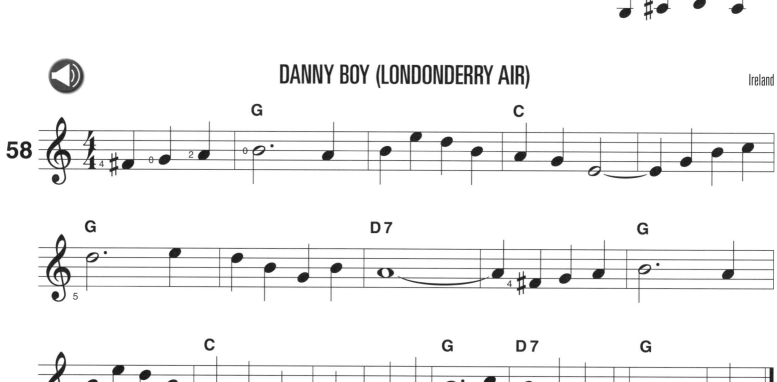

DANNY BOY (LONDONDERRY AIR)

Ireland

KEY SIGNATURES

Instead of writing a sharp sign before every F in a song, one sharp is placed at the beginning of the line. This is called a **key signature** and indicates that every F in the song should be played as F#. In "Shenandoah" there will be an arrow above each F# to remind you to play F#.

SHENANDOAH

Sea Shanty

Oh Shen - an - doah ___ I long to see you, ___ A -

way ___ you roll - ing riv - er, ___ Oh Shen - an - doah ___

___ I long to see you, ___ A - way ___ we're bound a -

way ___ a - cross the wide Miss - ou - ri.

SPY RIFF

SLOW/FAST

RESTS

Musical **rests** are moments of silence in music. Each type of note has a matching rest which has the same name and receives the same number of counts.

Whole	Half	Quarter
4 beats	2 beats	1 beat

A rest often requires that you stop the sound of your guitar strings with your right hand as is shown in the photo to the right. This process is called **dampening** the strings. Use the edge of your right palm to touch the strings, and work for little unnecessary movement.

As you play the following exercises that contain both notes and rests, count aloud using numbers for the notes and say the word, "rest," for each beat of silence.

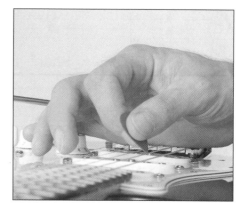

COUNT: 1   2   3   Rest   1   Rest   3   Rest   Rest   2   3   4   1 - 2   Rest   Rest

The letter **R** is used in place of the word "rest."

1   2   R   R   R   2   3   4   R   R   R   R   1   R   3   4   1 - 2 - 3   R

DEEP BLUE

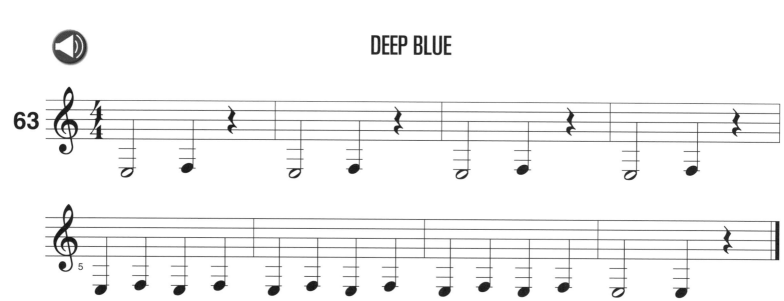

RED RIVER VALLEY

Cowboy Song

Come and sit by my side if you love me.

Do not has - ten to bid me a - dieu.

But re - mem - ber the Red Riv - er Val - ley,

and the cow - boy who loved you so true. _____

TWANG

In $\frac{3}{4}$ a complete measure of rest (3 counts) is written as a whole rest (—).

ROCK 'N' REST

EIGHTH NOTES

An **eighth note** is half the length of a quarter note and receives half a beat in $\frac{4}{4}$ or $\frac{3}{4}$ meter.

One eighth note is written with a flag. Consecutive eighth notes are connected with a beam.

To count eighth notes, divide the beat into two, and use "and" between the beats. Count the measure to the right aloud while tapping your foot on the beat.

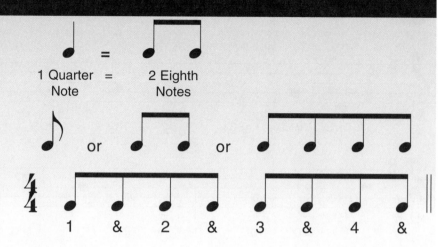

Eighth notes are played with a **downstroke** (⊓) of the pick on the beat and an **upstroke** (∨) on the "and." This is called **alternate picking**.

Play the following exercise using alternate picking for all eighth notes and strictly downstrokes for all quarter notes. Practice slowly and steadily at first; then gradually increase the speed.

A double bar with two dots (:|) is a **repeat sign**, and it tells you to play the music a second time.

SEA SHANTY

FRÉRE JACQUES

France

Fré - re   Jac - ques,   Fré - re   Jac - ques,   dor - mez vous?   Dor - mez vous?
Are you sleep - ing?   Are you sleep - ing?   Broth - er   John,   Broth - er   John,

Son - nez les ma - tin - es,   son - nez les ma - tin - es,   din, din, don;   din, din, don.
Morn - ing bells are ring - ing,   morn - ing bells are ring-ing,   ding, dong, ding;   ding, dong, ding.

SNAKE CHARMER

Try playing "Snake Charmer" again, this time on the higher strings. Begin an octave higher with the A note on the second fret of the third string, and use your ear as a guide.

THE STAR-SPANGLED BANNER

Key/Smith

MORE STRUMMING

The alternating down-up stroke pattern you have already played on eighth notes can also be applied to strumming. As you practice the following exercise, keep your wrist relaxed and flexible. The down-up motion will be much faster and easier if you use motion of the wrist only, rather than of the entire arm. This wrist motion feels a little like shaking water off the hand.

BASIC DOWN-UP STRUM

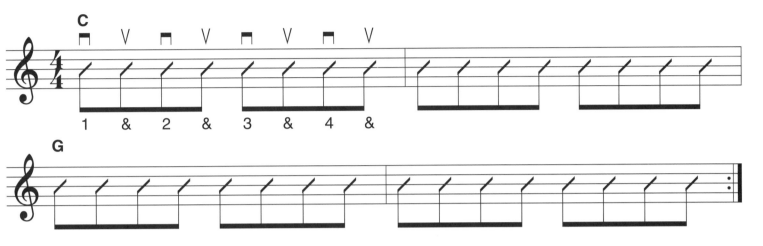

STRUM VARIATIONS

A variation of the basic down-up strum misses the upstroke or "and" of the first beat. Remember to keep the down-up motion going and miss the strings on the "and" of beat one.

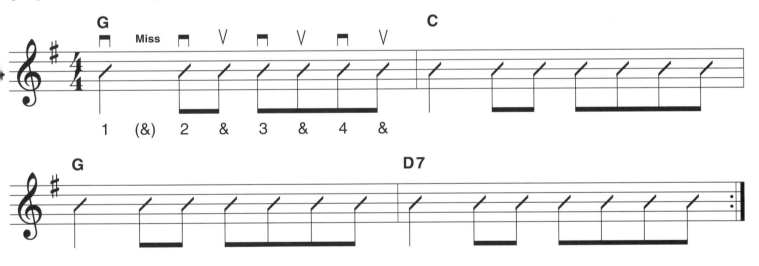

This variation misses two upstrokes. Continue to strum but miss the strings on the "and" of beats one and three.

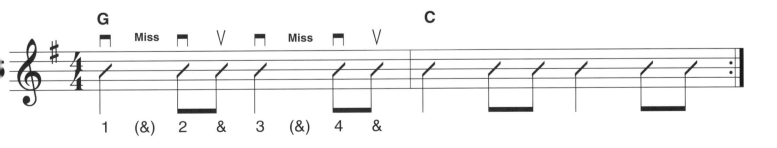

THE Em CHORD

Em

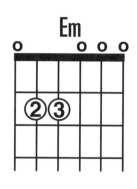

The E minor chord is one of the easiest chords on the guitar. Arch your fingers and play on the tips to avoid touching the other open strings.

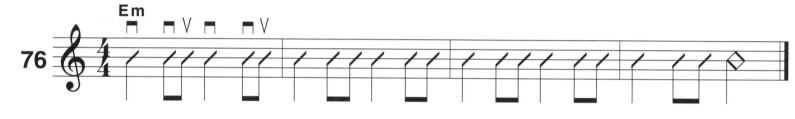

HEY, HO, NOBODY HOME

England

Hey, ho, no - bod - y home. Meat, nor drink, nor mon - ey have I none, yet will I be mer - ry. (ry.)

SHALOM CHAVERIM
(Peace, My Friend)

Israel

Sha - lom, cha - ve - rim! Sha - lom, cha - ve - rim! Sha - lom, sha - lom! Le - hit - ra - ot, le - hit - ra - ot. Sha - lom, sha - lom.

CHORD PAIRS

As you move between different chords, if one or more fingers remain on the same note, allow them to stay pressed as you switch chords. In the following progression, there is a common finger between the G and Em chords and a common finger between the C and D7 chords.

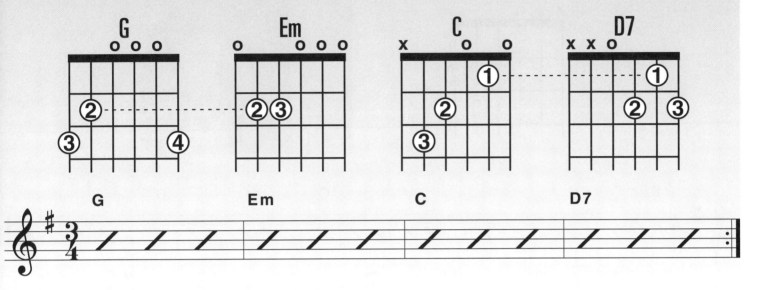

Practice the following chord progressions until you can play them steadily and without any hesitation between chord changes. Try to move your fingers to a new chord as a unit instead of "letting your fingers do the walking" one at a time.

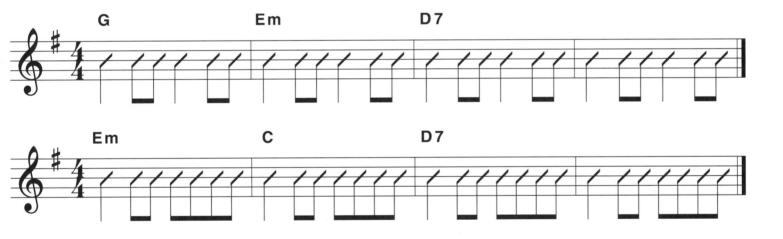

You can vary the strumming by alternating between a bass note (usually the lowest note of a chord and the name of the chord) and the remainder of the chord. This style of accompaniment is referred to as the **bass note strum**, or "boom chick" rhythm.

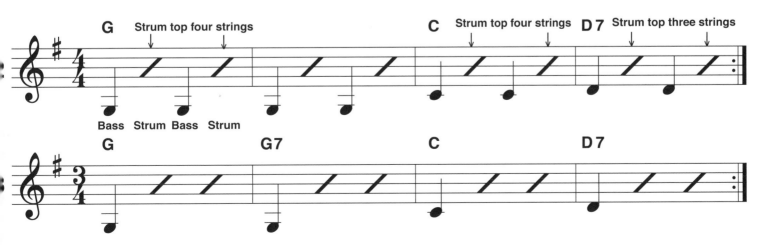

THE D CHORD

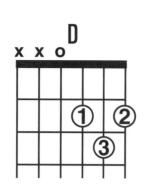

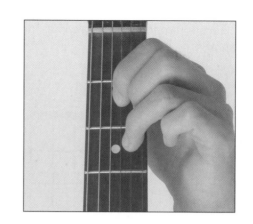

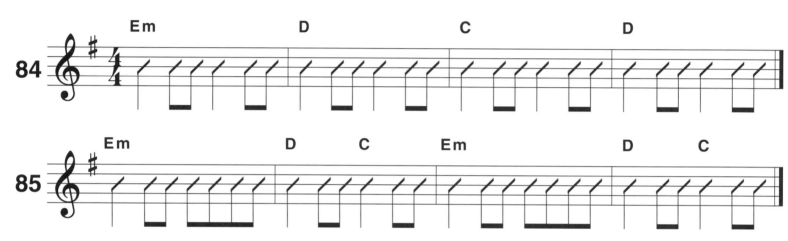

THIS TRAIN

African American

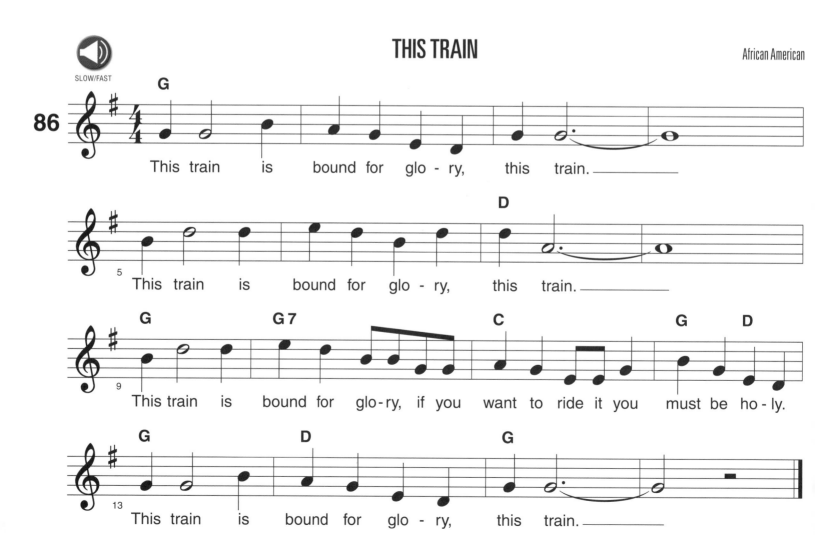

This train is bound for glo - ry, this train.

This train is bound for glo - ry, this train.

This train is bound for glo - ry, if you want to ride it you must be ho - ly.

This train is bound for glo - ry, this train.

BOOGIE BASS

The next example uses a variation on the bass note strum technique. This time, strike the bass note and then strum the remainder of the chord twice.

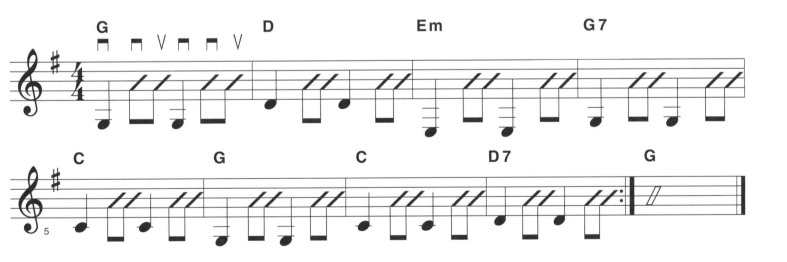

Practice these strums before playing "Simple Gifts."

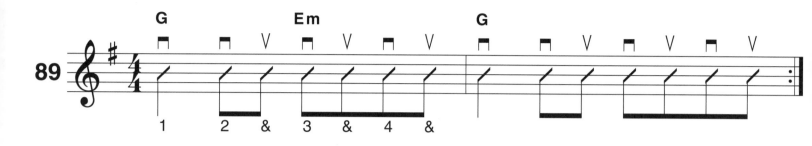

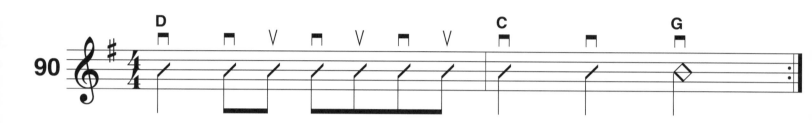

On "Simple Gifts" you can play the melody (Part 1), the harmony line (Part 2), or the chordal accompaniment.

SIMPLE GIFTS

Shaker Song

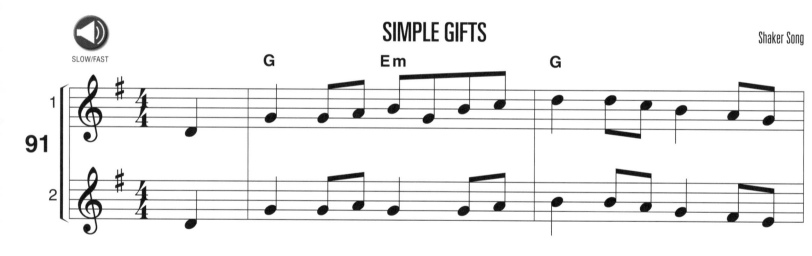

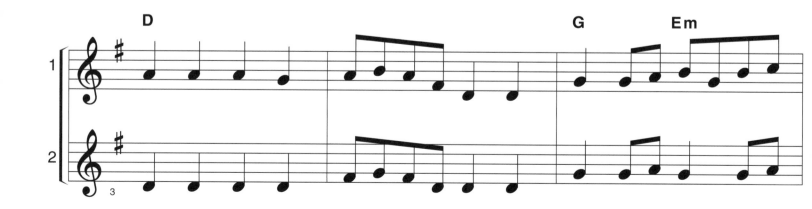

C-SHARP (C#)

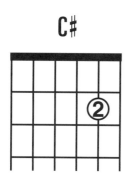

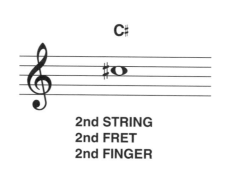

C#

2nd STRING
2nd FRET
2nd FINGER

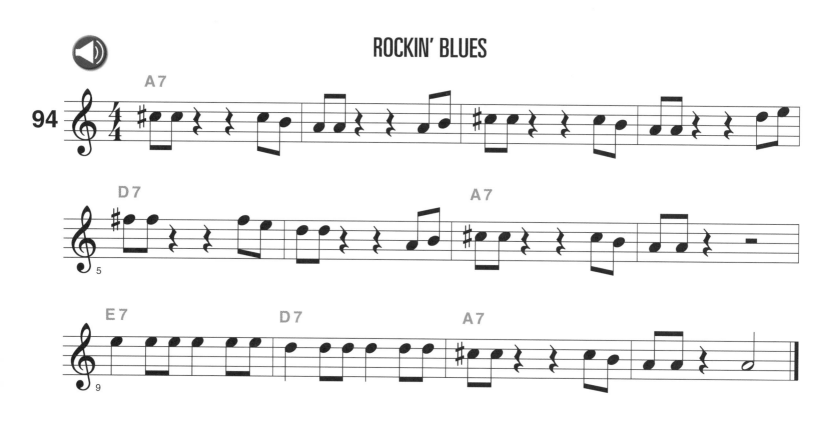

ROCKIN' BLUES

THE A7 CHORD

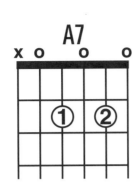

A7

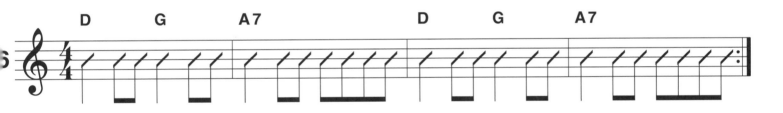

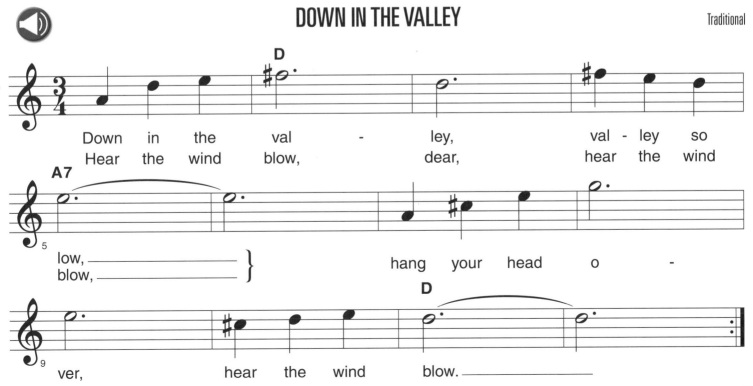

DOWN IN THE VALLEY

Traditional

Down in the val - ley, val - ley so
Hear the wind blow, dear, hear the wind

low, _____ } hang your head o -
blow, _____

ver, hear the wind blow. _____

43

MINUET IN G

J.S. BACH

98

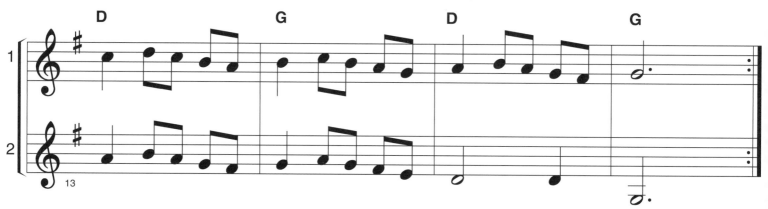

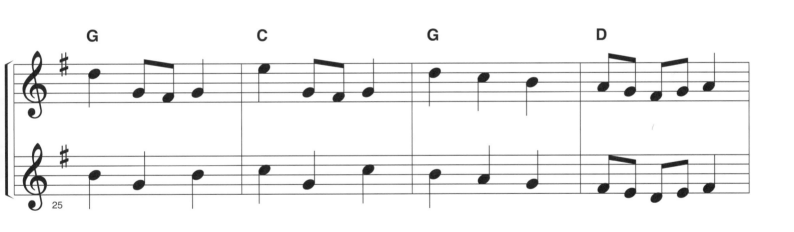

Repeat to top of page

TIME IS ON MY SIDE

Jerry Ragovoy

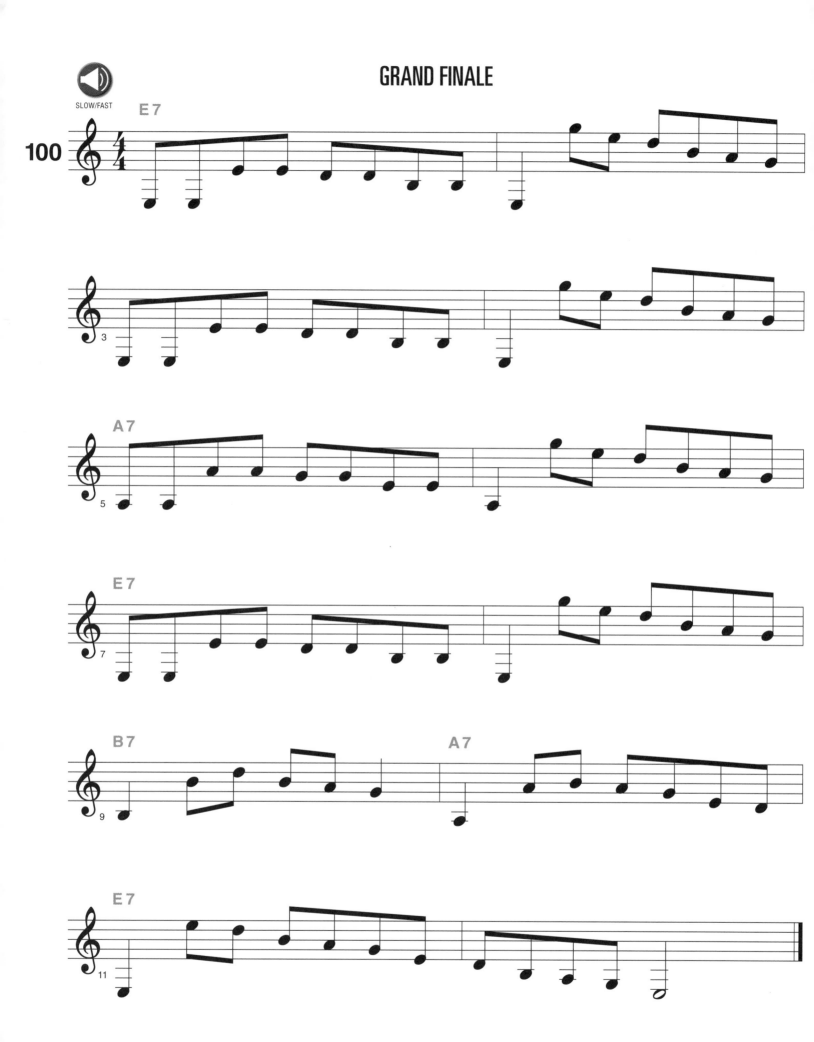

GRAND FINALE

SLOW/FAST

100

CHORD CHART

In this chart you will find the chords learned in this book as well as several other common chords you may see in music you are playing.

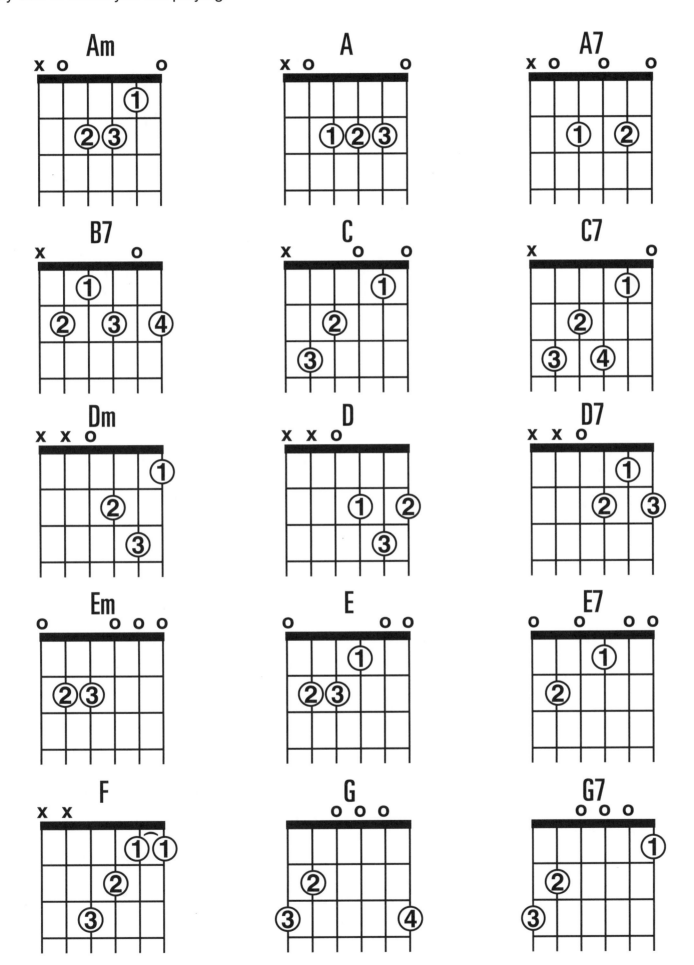

THE Am CHORD

Am
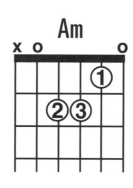

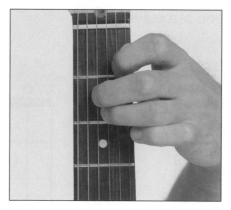

Practice changing chords in the following examples. Play slowly and steadily so there is no hesitation between chords.

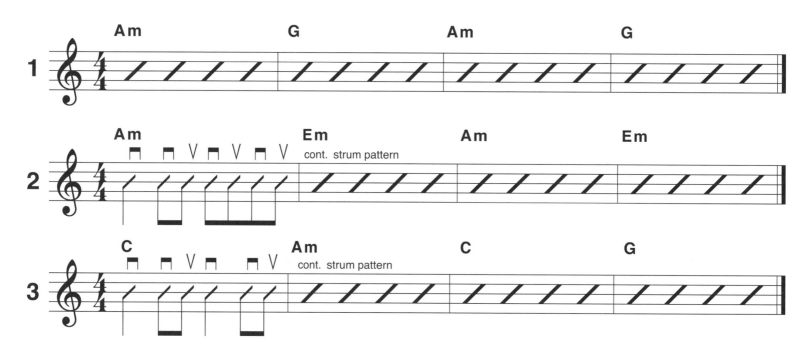

1   Am   G   Am   G

2   Am   Em   Am   Em   cont. strum pattern

3   C   Am   C   G   cont. strum pattern

SINNER MAN

Traditional

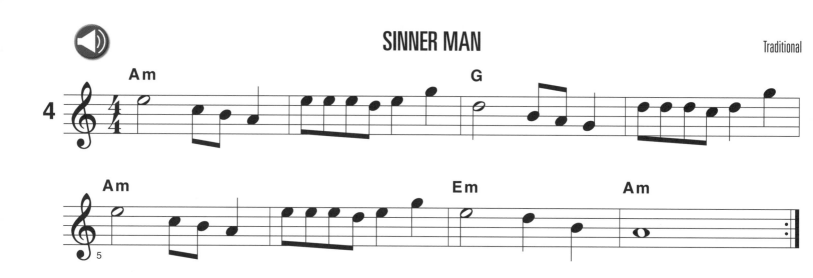

DOTTED QUARTER NOTES

You've already learned that a dot after a note increases the value by one half.

$$\text{2 beats} \quad + \quad \text{1 beat} \quad = \quad \text{3 beats}$$

A dot after a quarter note also increases its value by one half.

$$\text{1 beat} \quad + \quad \tfrac{1}{2} \text{ beat} \quad = \quad 1\tfrac{1}{2} \text{ beats}$$

Practice the riffs below, which use dotted quarter notes.

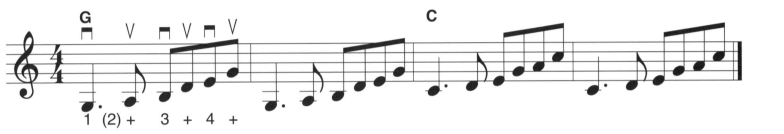

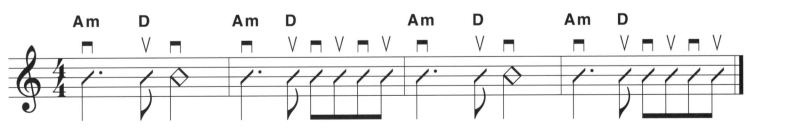

51

THE Dm CHORD

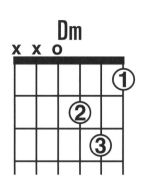

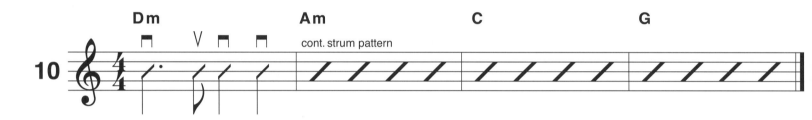

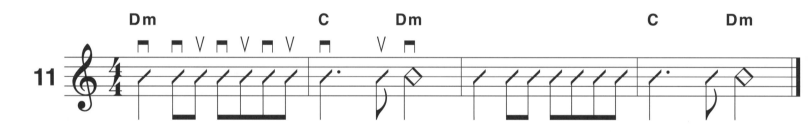

EIGHTH REST

The equivalent rest for an eighth note looks like this:

$$\eighthnote = \text{𝄾}$$

You can either lift your left-hand fingers off the chord or dampen the strings with your right hand.

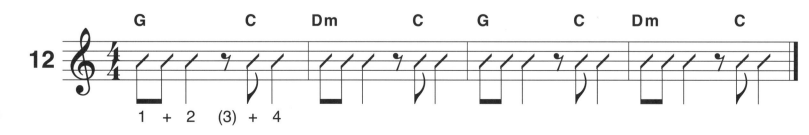

SYNCOPATION

Syncopation is the stressing or accenting of notes on the "ands" of beats. The accent may be a result of tying eighth notes together or of placing quarter notes on the off-beats.

Use alternate picking throughout the following exercises. When you see a count in parentheses, simply miss the string and let the sound ring. By doing this you will play the syncopated pattern with the correct stroke of the pick.

Following are two common syncopated strum patterns. Practice these with various chords.

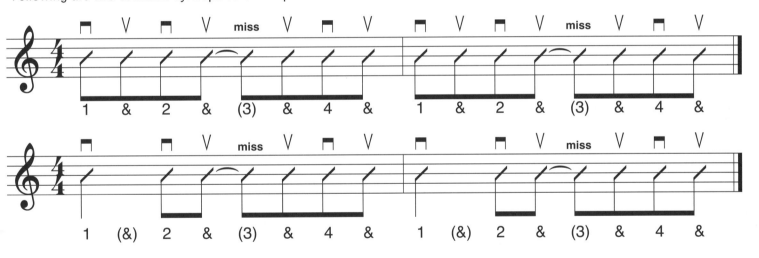

JOSHUA FOUGHT THE BATTLE OF JERICHO

African-American Spiritual

SLOW/FAST

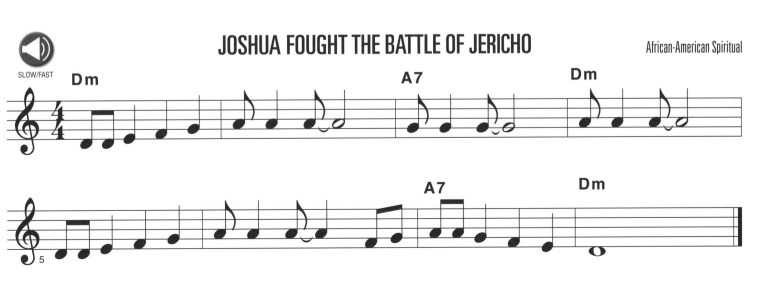

First play the melody; then sing as you strum the chords for the next song.

ROCK-A-MY SOUL

African-American Spiritual

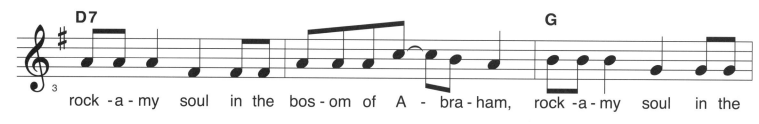

Rock - a - my soul in the bos - om of A - bra - ham,

rock - a - my soul in the bos - om of A - bra - ham, rock - a - my soul in the

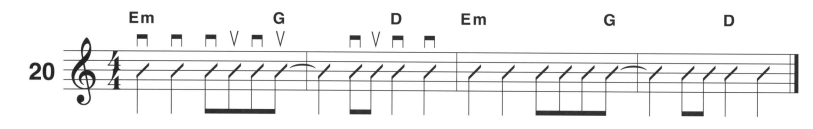

bos - om of A - bra - ham, oh, rock - a - my soul.

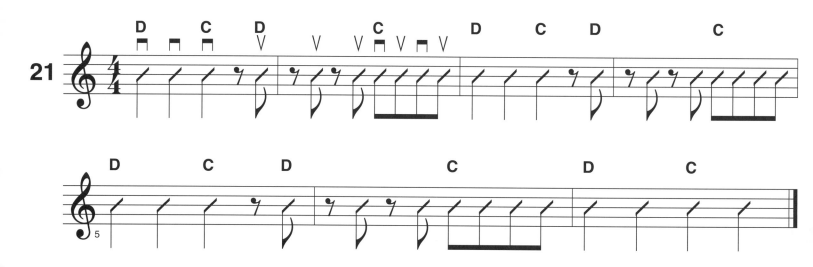

Release your left-hand pressure when an eighth rest is indicated in the next example.

54

JAMAICA FAREWELL

Traditional Caribbean

THE A CHORD

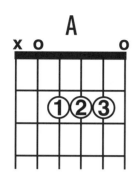

A

x o   o

① ② ③

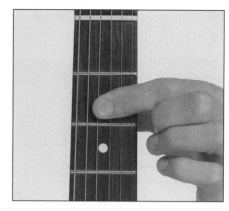

Optional Fingering (string 1 is not played)

On the next example, try muting the strings on each rest with your left-hand fingers.

Here is another type of muting effect. As you strum the muted chord (X), touch the strings with your palm a split second before you strike them with your pick.

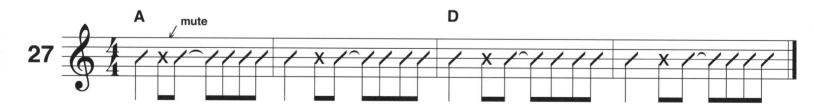

WHAT'S A KEY

The **key** is another name for a tonal center of a song. Songs usually end on their key note. So far, you have played in the keys of C (no sharps or flats) and G (one sharp).

THE KEY OF D

The key signature for D has an F-sharp and a C-sharp. All Fs and Cs should be played one half step (fret) higher.

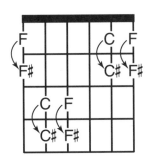

OH, MARY DON'T YOU WEEP

Traditional Spiritual

FOURTH FINGER WORKOUT

Build up the muscles in your fourth finger by playing these exercises.

A **natural** sign (♮) cancels a sharp in the key signature for the remainder of the measure.

DE COLORES

Mexican Folk Song

29

All _____ the col-ors, all the col-ors that bloom in the
De _____ co - lo - res, de co - lo - res se vis - ten los

mead-ows are col-ors of spring - time. _____
cam - pos en la pri - ma - ve - ra. _____

All _____ the col - ors, all the col-ors that dance in the
De _____ co - lo - res, de co - lo - res son los pa-ja-

sky are the col-ors of rain - bows. _____
ri - tos que vie-nen de a fue - ra. _____

All _____ the col - ors, all the col-ors of na-ture spring
De _____ co - lo - res, de co - lo - res es el ar - co

forth to make my heart sing. Then I know why the col - ors of
i - ris que ve - mos lu - cir, y por e - so los gran-des a -

spring-time are bring-ing me joy and a heart full of love.
mo - res de mu - chos co - lo - res me gus - tan a mí.

ENDINGS

The following song has a first and second ending indicated by brackets with the numbers 1 and 2.

When you reach the repeat sign (:‖) in the first ending, go back to the beginning or initial repeat sign (‖:). On the second time through, skip the first ending and go on to the second ending.

ANGELS WE HAVE HEARD ON HIGH

Traditional French Carol

An - gels we have heard on high sweet - ly sing - ing o'er the plains,

and the moun - tains in re - ply ech - o - ing their joy - ous strains.

Glo - ri - a

in ex - cel - sis de - o, in ex - cel - sis de - o.

CATCHY RIFF

SLOW/FAST

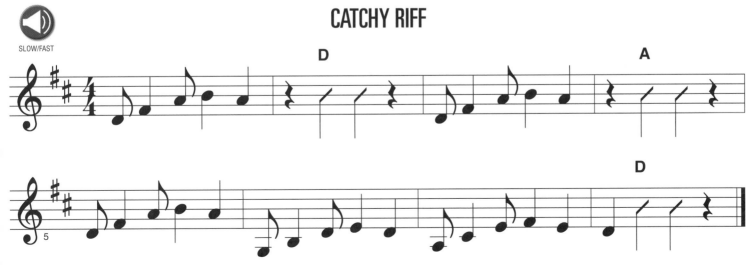

SECOND POSITION

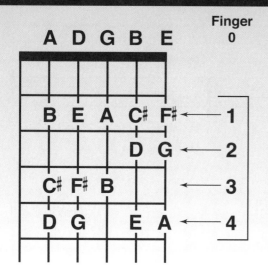

A D G B E	Finger 0
B E A C# F# ←	1
D G ←	2
C# F# B ←	3
D G E A ←	4

Throughout Book 1 and until now in Book 2 you have played in **first position**, with the first finger in the first fret, the second finger in the second fret, and so on. The name of your finger position is determined by where you place your first finger.

If the first finger is placed at the second fret as indicated by the diagram at the left, you will be playing in what is called **second position**. Fingers 2, 3, and 4 play in frets 3, 4, and 5 as indicated.

Notice that open notes can also be played in an alternate position on the fretboard.

The principal advantage of playing in the second position lies in the ease with which certain passages can be fingered.

Practice the song below in second position using both the open-string notes and their alternate fingerings on the fretboard.

MARIANNE

Caribbean

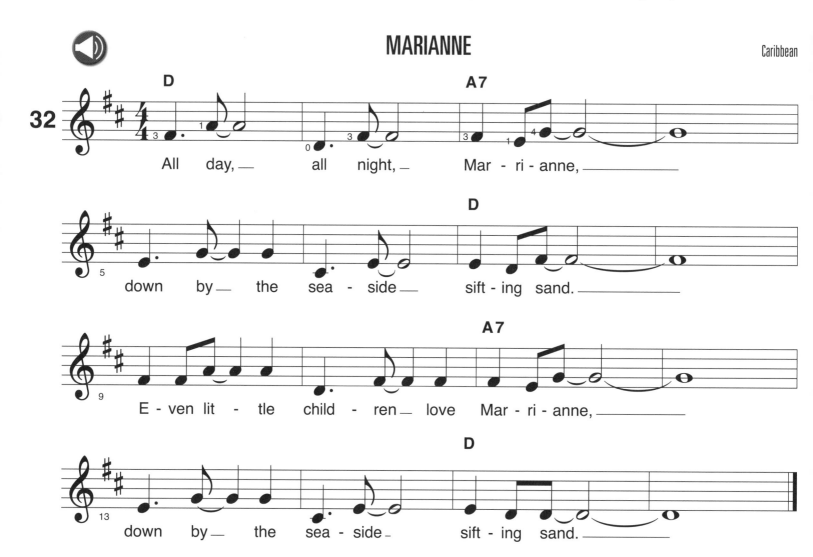

After playing the melody to "Marianne," try playing some of the syncopated strums you've already learned. You can also go back to pages 10 and 11 and play those melodies in second position.

Some songs are played in more than one position. The following piece shifts between first position and second position.

BLUES/ROCK RIFF

THE HIGH A NOTE

Play the new note, A, with your fourth finger in second position.

THE WABASH CANNONBALL

Hobo Song

D   **D7**   **G**

Lis - ten to the   jin - gle,   the   rum - ble and the   roar.

A7   **D**

Rid - ing through the   wood - lands   to the   hills and by the   shore.   Hear the

D7   **G**

might - y rush of the en - gine,   hear the   lone - some ho - bo   squall.

A7   **D**

Rid - ing through the   jun - gle   on the   Wa - bash Can - non - ball.

THE E CHORD

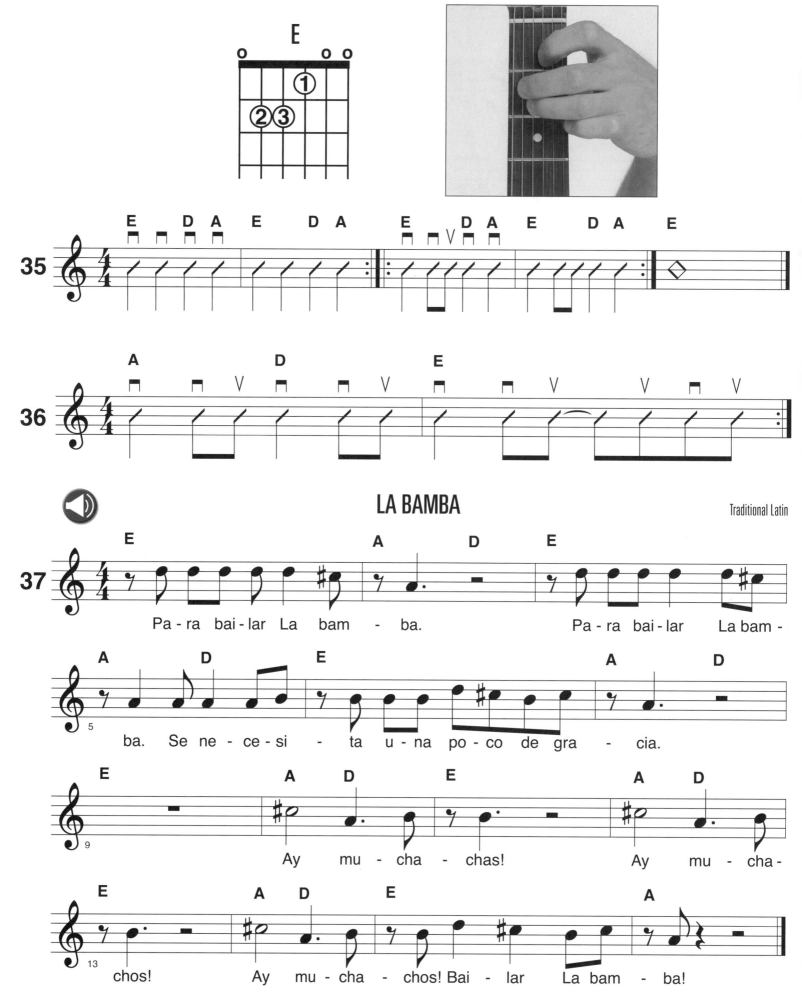

LA BAMBA

Traditional Latin

Pa - ra bai - lar La bam - ba. Pa - ra bai - lar La bam - ba. Se ne - ce - si - ta u - na po - co de gra - cia. Ay mu - cha - chas! Ay mu - cha - chos! Ay mu - cha - chos! Bai - lar La bam - ba!

THE KEY OF A

The key signature for A has three sharps: F-sharp, C-sharp, and G-sharp. Study the diagram below to learn where the new G# notes are played.

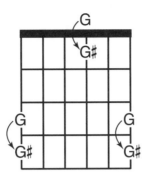

Play "Joy to the World" in second position.

JOY TO THE WORLD

Handel

POWER CHORDS

The **power chord** is commonly used in rock and other contemporary music. Most chords have three or more notes; power chords have just two. Also, notice that power chords are labeled with the suffix "5."

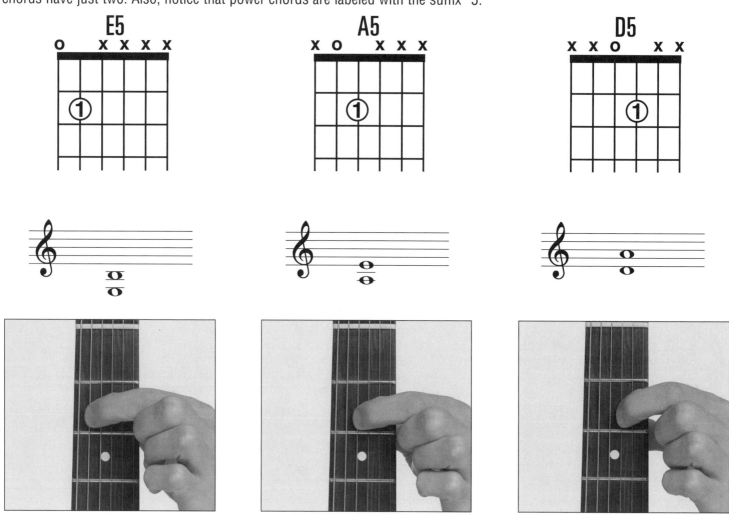

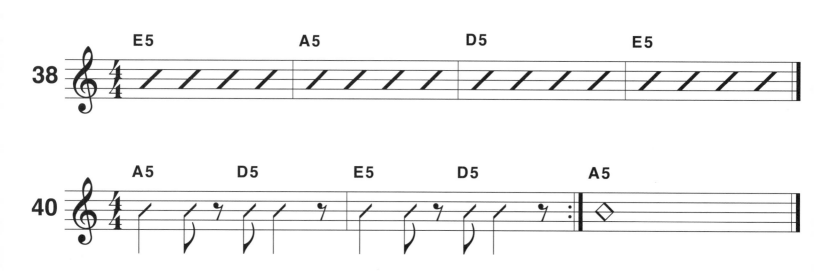

TABLATURE

Tablature graphically represents the guitar fingerboard. Each horizontal line represents a string, and each number represents a fret.

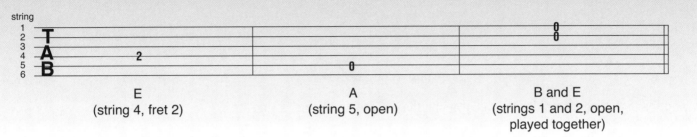

E
(string 4, fret 2)

A
(string 5, open)

B and E
(strings 1 and 2, open,
played together)

The same information is given on the musical staff and in tablature. Practice reading both.

STEADY GROOVE

SLOW/FAST

THE SHUFFLE

In traditional styles like blues and jazz, eighth notes are played unevenly. Play the first note twice as long as the second.

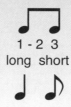

Playing the eighth notes in this way will give you the desired shuffle or "swing" feel.

POWER CHORD SHUFFLE

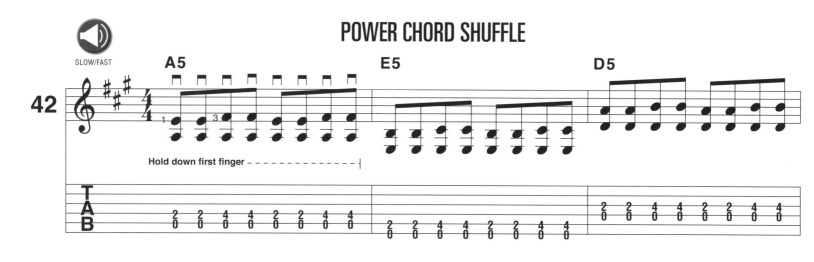

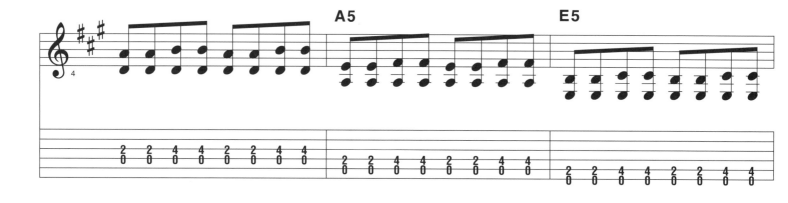

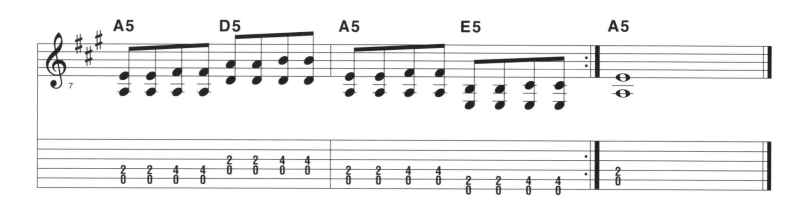

Practice the following song using the power chord shuffle accompaniment you just learned. Or, play the melody using the shuffle rhythm.

MIDNIGHT SPECIAL

Prison Song

Verse

Well you wake up in the morn - ing, — hear the ding - dong ring, — Go march - ing to the ta - ble, — see the same darn thing, Knife and fork are on the ta - ble — noth - in' in my pan, — And if you say a thing a - bout it, — you're in trou - ble with the

Chorus

man. Let the mid - night spe - cial, — shine its light on — you. —

Let the mid - night spe - cial — shine its ev - er lov - in' light on you.

 Try playing "Midnight Special" again using an even eighth note rock feel.

THE BLUES

The blues style was originated in the early 1900s by African Americans from the Mississippi Delta. Blues became an important ingredient in jazz, country, rock, and other forms of popular music.

The most typical blues is twelve measures (bars) long. Many **12-bar blues** follow this chord progression below. Use the power chord shuffle you have just learned.

C.C. RIDER

Traditional

C. C. rid - er, ___ see what you have done. ___
Tell me rid - er, ___ what is on your mind. ___

C. C. rid - er, see what you have done. ___ You
Tell me rid - er, what is on your mind. ___ Oh,

made me love you, now your friend has come. ___
tell me why you treat me so un - kind. ___

SHUFFLE RIFF

THE KEY OF Am

The **key of A minor** has a key signature of no sharps or flats. A minor is called the **relative minor** of C major because it shares the same parent key signature. The relative minor always begins two notes lower than the major key (C-B-A).

"Wayfaring Stranger" is a well-known Sacred Harp spiritual from the Southern United States.

WAYFARING STRANGER

Sacred Harp Spiritual

When a G# is added to A natural minor, it is called the **harmonic minor**. Find all of the G# notes (one fret higher than G or one fret lower than A) before playing "Hava Nagila." Notice that "Hava Nagila" speeds up on the repeat then slows down on the last line.

HAVA NAGILA

Israeli Dance

FINGERSTYLE GUITAR

Fingerstyle, also known as fingerpicking, is a very popular style of guitar accompaniment which uses **arpeggios** (broken chords) instead of strummed chords. The distinctive sound of fingerpicking comes from the thumb and fingers plucking only one string each in succession.

The right-hand finger and thumb letters used in this book are based on the internationally accepted system of Spanish words and letters:

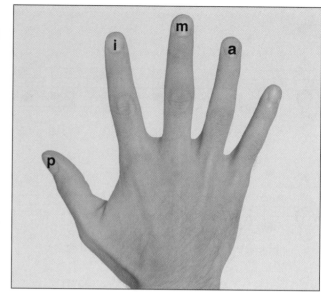

p	pulgar	=	thumb
i	indice	=	index finger
m	medio	=	middle finger
a	anular	=	ring finger

Follow these steps to learn how to fingerpick:

- The thumb (p) plucks strings 4, 5, and 6 depending upon which string is the bass or root of the chord. This motion is a downward stroke. Use the left side of the thumb and thumbnail.

- The other fingers (i, m, a) pluck the string in an upward stroke with the fleshy tip of the finger and fingernail.

- The index finger (i) always plucks string 3.

- The middle finger (m) always plucks string 2.

- The ring finger (a) always plucks string 1.

The thumb and each finger must pluck only one string per stroke and not brush over several strings. (This would be a strum.) Let the strings ring throughout the duration of the chord.

RIGHT-HAND POSITION

Use a high wrist; arch your palm as if you were holding a ping-pong ball. Keep the thumb outside and away from the fingers, and let the fingers do the work rather than lifting your whole hand. Study the photo at the right.

Practice the fingerpicking patterns below. Work toward an even sound on each string plucked.

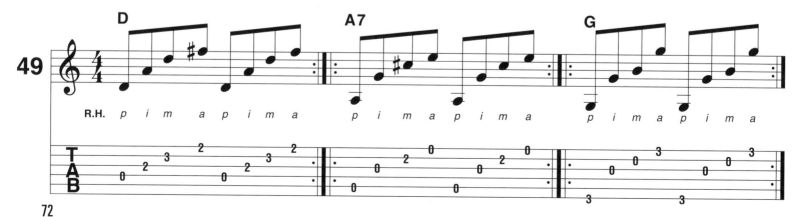

SWING LOW, SWEET CHARIOT

African-American Spiritual

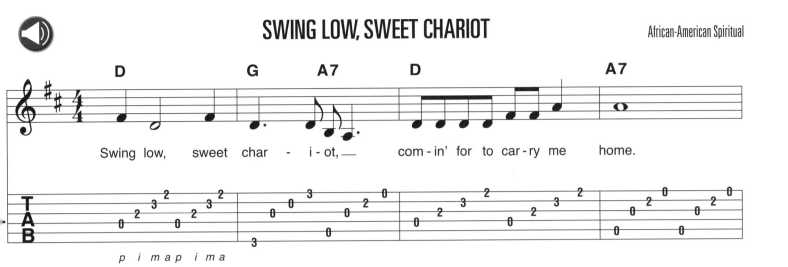

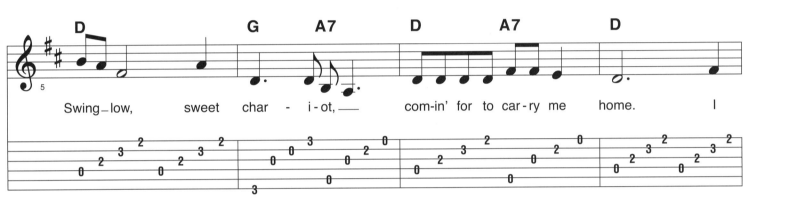

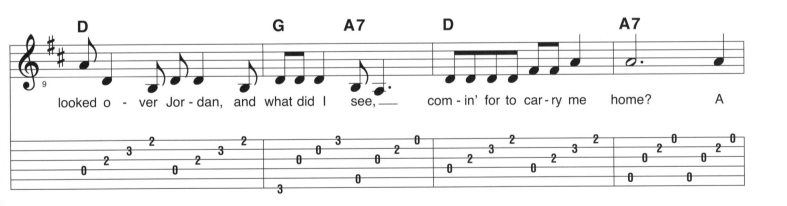

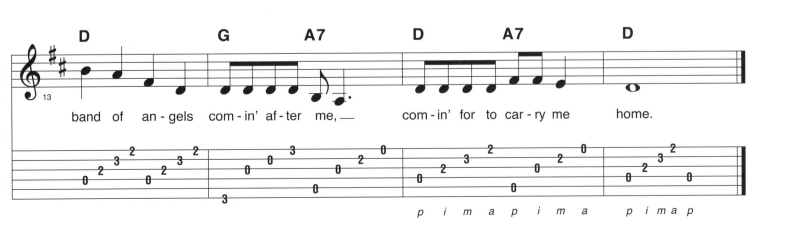

The fingerstyle pattern used in "Scarborough Fair" is commonly used for songs in $\frac{3}{4}$ time.

SCARBOROUGH FAIR

British Ballad

The fingerstyle accompaniment to "The Water Is Wide" uses two new chords, **Bm/A** (B minor with an A in the bass) and **Dsus2** (D with an open first string) that are easy to play. Study each chord frame below before playing the accompaniment.

THE WATER IS WIDE

English Folk Song

THE F CHORD

Unlike other chords you have played, the F chord has two strings depressed by one finger. The first finger forms a small **barre** across strings 1 and 2. You will find that it is easier to roll this finger slightly so that the strings are depressed by the outside rather than the flat underside of the first finger.

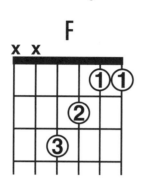

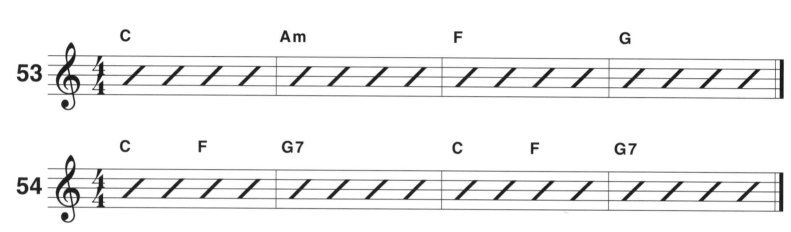

Another option for playing arpeggios is to use a pick. Try this on the next song.

PICKING CHORDS

Play the accompaniment to "House of the Rising Sun" either with a pick or fingerstyle.

HOUSE OF THE RISING SUN

American Ballad

CARTER STYLE SOLOS

Carter style solos are a famous guitar style popularized by Country music legend Maybelle Carter of the Carter family. The melody is played on the lower strings and the spaces between the melody are filled by strummed partial chords. Emphasize the melody notes and play lightly on the strums.

ROW, ROW, ROW YOUR BOAT

Traditional

MAN OF CONSTANT SORROW

Southern U.S. Ballad

SLOW/FAST

WILDWOOD FLOWER

Appalachan Folk Song

BASS RUNS

A **bass run** is a pattern of notes that connects the bass notes of two chords. The bass run gives your accompaniment variety and provides momentum toward the new chord. Practice these bass runs between G and C or G and D; then play them with the bluegrass classic, "Goin' Down the Road."

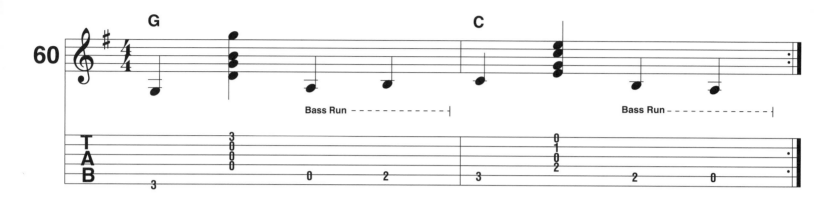

An optional form of the G to C run replaces the second beat strum with another bass note.

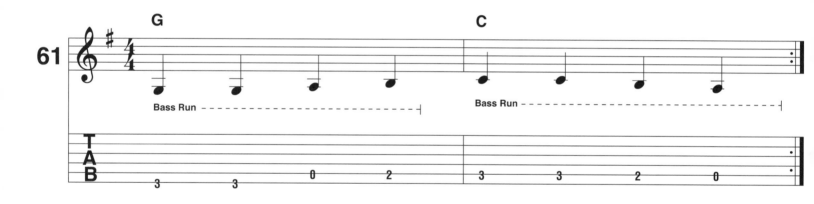

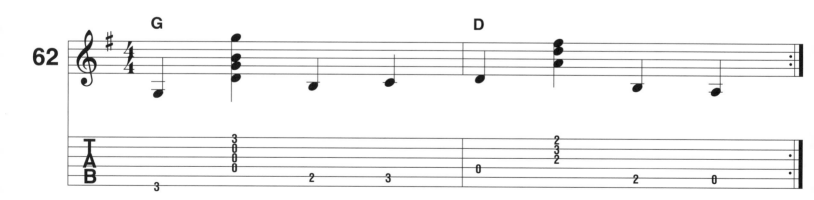

GOIN' DOWN THE ROAD

2. I'm goin' where those chilly winds don't blow *(3 times)*
   I ain't gonna be treated this a-way.

3. I'm goin' where the water tastes like wine *(3 times)*
   I ain't gonna be treated this a-way.

THE B7 CHORD

B7 is your first four-finger chord. Notice that the second-fret fingers are placed on strings 1, 3, and 5. Keeping this visual pattern in mind will help you move to this chord quickly.

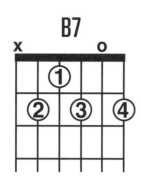

When you change from E or Em to B7, keep your second finger down.

WE THREE KINGS

Traditional

We three kings of Or - i - ent are. Bear - ing

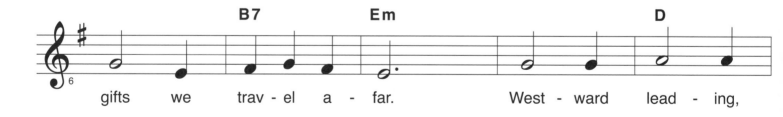

gifts we trav - el a - far. West - ward lead - ing,

still pro - ceed - ing, guide us to yon - der star.

THE KEY OF E

On the guitar, the key of E sounds good. It is an ideal key for both singing and playing.

The key signature for E has four sharps: F-sharp, C-sharp, G-sharp, and D-sharp. Study the diagram below to learn where the new D♯ notes are played.

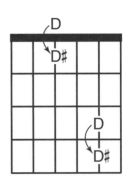

BY THE WATERS OF BABYLON

Caribbean

By the wat - ers of Bab - y - lon, where we sat down,

And there we wept _____ when we re - mem - bered Zi - on. _____

BATTLE HYMN OF THE REPUBLIC

Civil War

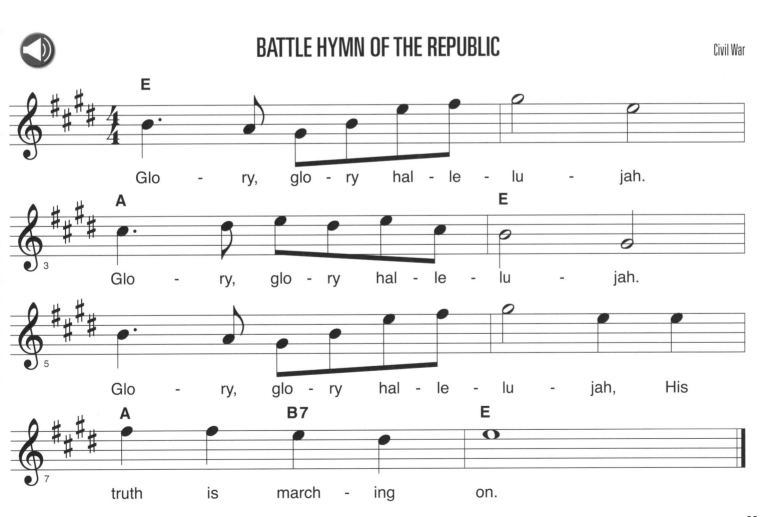

Glo - ry, glo - ry hal - le - lu - jah.

Glo - ry, glo - ry hal - le - lu - jah.

Glo - ry, glo - ry hal - le - lu - jah, His

truth is march - ing on.

TRIPLETS

Triplets subdivide a unit into three parts instead of two parts. In $\frac{4}{4}$ or $\frac{3}{4}$ time, two eighth notes get one count, so an eighth-note triplet will also get one count.

Triplets are beamed together with a number 3. To count a triplet, simply say the word "tri-pl-et" during one beat. Tap your foot to the beat, and count aloud:

COUNT: 1   2   tri-pi-let   4   tri-pi-let   tri-pi-let   3   4   1   2   &   tri-pi-let   4

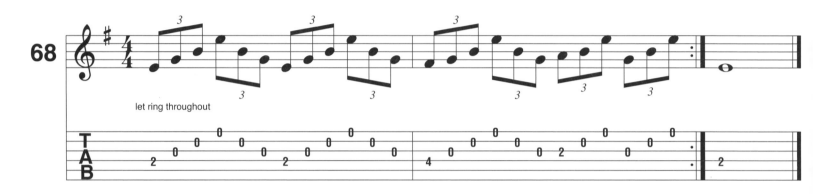

68

let ring throughout

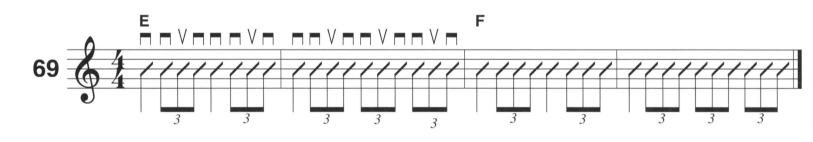

69

E   F

JESU, JOY OF MAN'S DESIRING

Bach

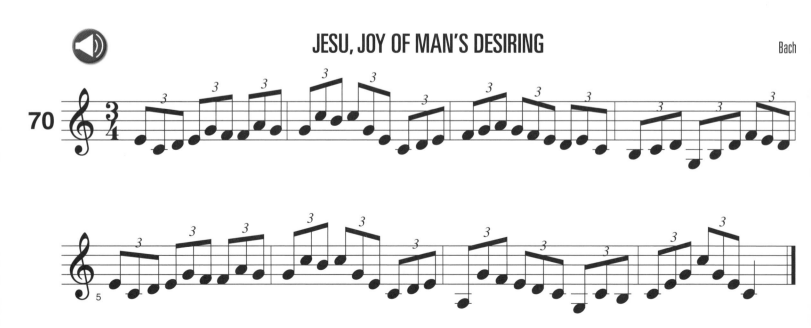

70

DEEP BLUES

Triplets can also be applied to a 12-bar blues. Play the following piece in second position.

LOST IN THE SHUFFLE

THE PENTATONIC SCALE

Pentatonic scales are widely used in styles ranging from blues, rock, and country to various world musics. The easiest pentatonic (five-note scale) to play on the guitar includes the notes E, G, A, B, and D. If you start this scale on E, it is called the E **minor pentatonic**. If you start it on G (relative major) it is called the G **major pentatonic**.

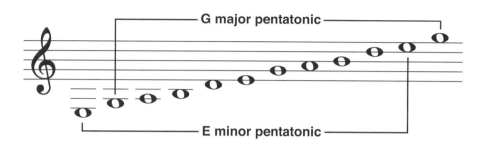

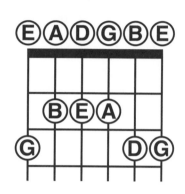

ROCK LICK

COUNTRY/ROCK LICK

HARD ROCK LICK

BLUEGRASS LICK

COUNTRY LICK

BLUES LICK

ROCK 'N' ROLL LICK

BLUES/ROCK LICK

PENTATONIC LEAD GUITAR

IMPROVISING

Use the E minor pentatonic you just learned to play solo leads over a 12-bar blues in E. If you don't have the recording, take turns playing rhythm and leads with friends or record your own rhythm tracks and play lead over them.

IMPROV TIPS

- **Hang Around Home** – Base your solo around the root (letter name) of the chord being played.

- **Less Is More** – Choose your notes carefully; sometimes it's not the quantity; it's the quality.

- **Work the Rhythm** – Use syncopations, triplets, and repeating patterns to help make your solos interesting and distinctive.

- **Tell a Story** – Let your solo take shape with a beginning, middle, and end.

OPEN JAM

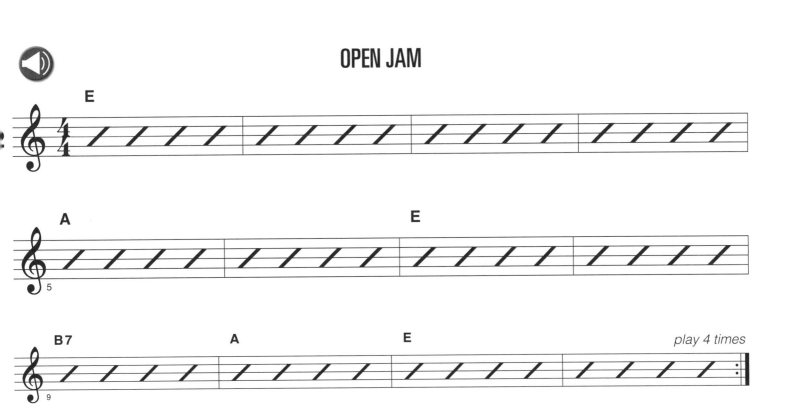

MOVABLE POWER CHORDS

So far, you have learned three power chords (E5, A5, and D5) that use an open string and first finger. Now use your first and third fingers to form a power chord that can be moved up and down the fingerboard.

The movable power chord shapes below are named by where the first finger is placed on the fretboard. You can use either strings 6 and 5 or strings 5 and 4 to play these chords.

SIXTH STRING ROOT

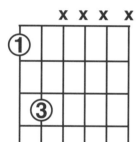

FIFTH STRING ROOT

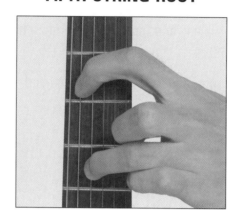

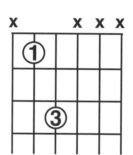

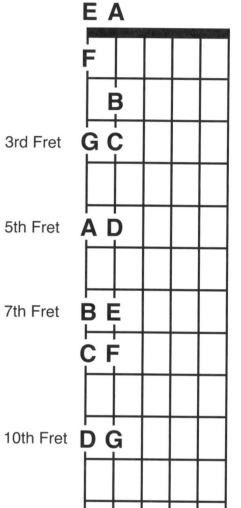

Study the fingerboard chart at the right to identify the letter names of natural notes on strings 6 and 5. If you want to play C5, locate C on either string 6 or string 5 and apply the correct shape from above. Move to D5 by simply sliding up two frets. That's the logic behind movable chords.

POP RIFF

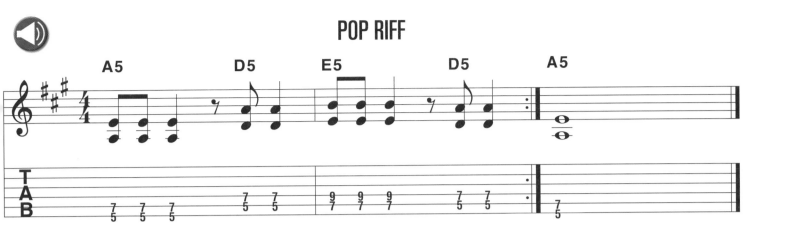

EARLY ROCK RIFF

HARD ROCK RIFF

POP/ROCK RIFF

The next example uses both movable power chords and an open-position power chord you learned earlier in the book.

Now try two riffs that mix power chords with single notes.

PALM MUTING

Palm muting is a technique in which you allow the side or heel of your picking hand to rest against the bridge, muffling or "muting" the strings as you play. Use this technique when you see the abbreviation "P.M." under the notes (between the staff and tab).

Palm muting sounds especially good with power chords and some amp distortion. Try this when playing the next two examples.

MUTED GROOVE

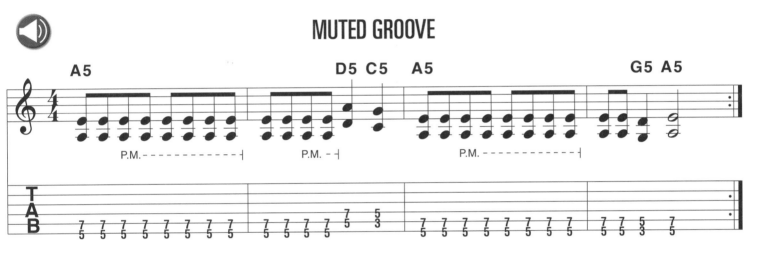

An **accent mark** (>) written above or below a note or chord indicates to play that note or chord slightly louder than the others.

ACCENTED RHYTHM

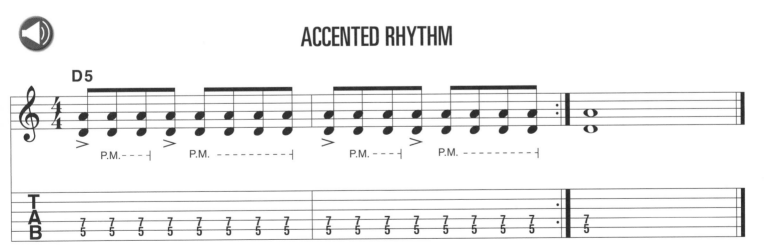

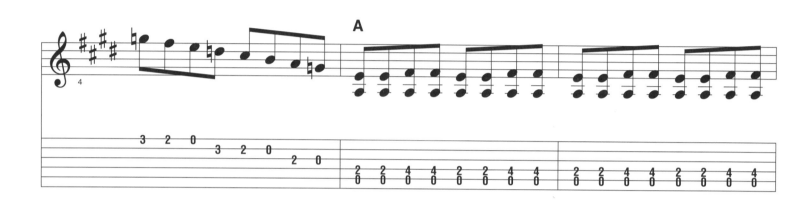

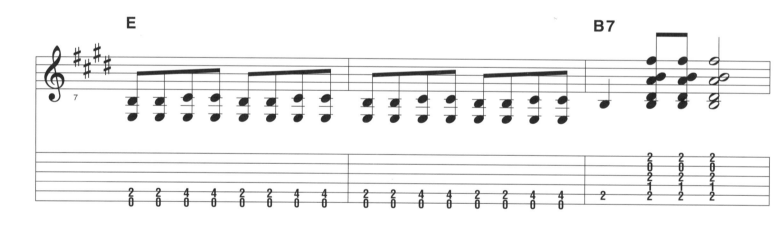

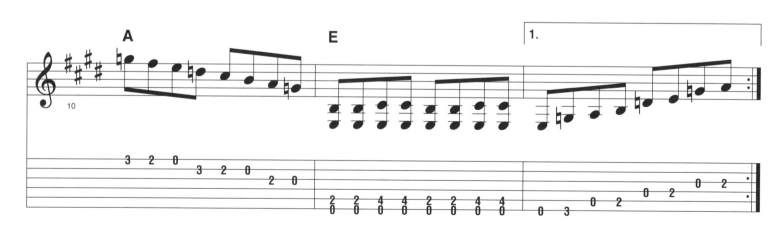

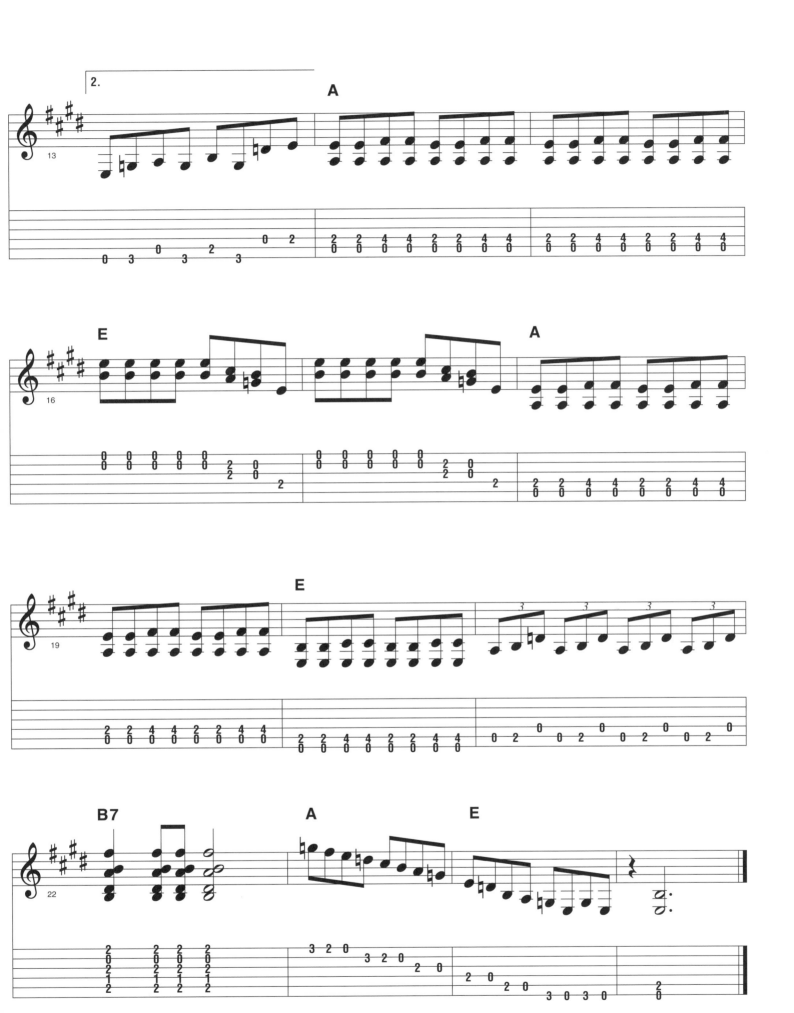

THE MAJOR SCALE

A **scale** is a series of notes arranged in a specific order. Perhaps the most common scale is the **major scale**. It is used as the basis for countless melodies, riffs, solos, and chord progressions.

Scales are constructed using a combination of whole steps and half steps. (Remember: on the guitar, a half step is the distance of one fret; a whole step is two frets.) All major scales are built from the following step pattern.

WHOLE — WHOLE — HALF — WHOLE — WHOLE — WHOLE — HALF

This series of whole and half steps gives the major scale its characteristic sound.

C MAJOR SCALE

To build a C major scale, start with the note C and follow the step pattern from above.

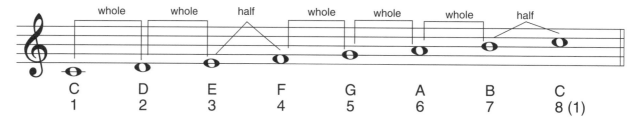

The first (and eighth) degree of a major scale is called the keynote or **tonic**. This is the "home" tone on which most melodies end.

Practice the C major scale ascending and descending in first position.

Try this: start on second string, first fret C and play a major scale up the second string using the pattern of whole and half steps.

Chords and chord progressions are also derived from scales. A piece of music based on the C major scale is in the key of C major. For every key, there are seven corresponding chords—one built on each note of the major scale.

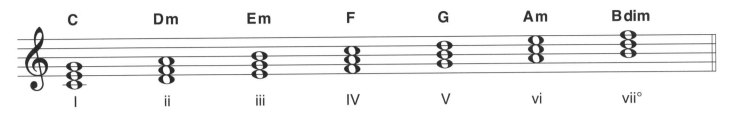

Note: Triads (three-note chords) use every other note of a scale (1-3-5, 2-4-6, etc.). Roman numerals are used to label a chord's location within a key.

By taking a closer look at each of the seven chords, notice that major triads are built on the first, fourth, and fifth notes of the scale; minor triads are built on the second, third, and sixth notes of the scale; and a diminished triad is built on the seventh note of the scale. The seven chords are common to the key of C because all seven contain only the notes of the C major scale (no sharps or flats). It is important to memorize this sequence of chord types, as it applies to all major scales.

The following examples are in the key of C. Practice playing the chords; then try improvising using the C major scale. When beginning to improvise, play the scale ascending and descending and notice how the notes work over the chords. Then, mix up the notes. It helps to emphasize the chord tones.

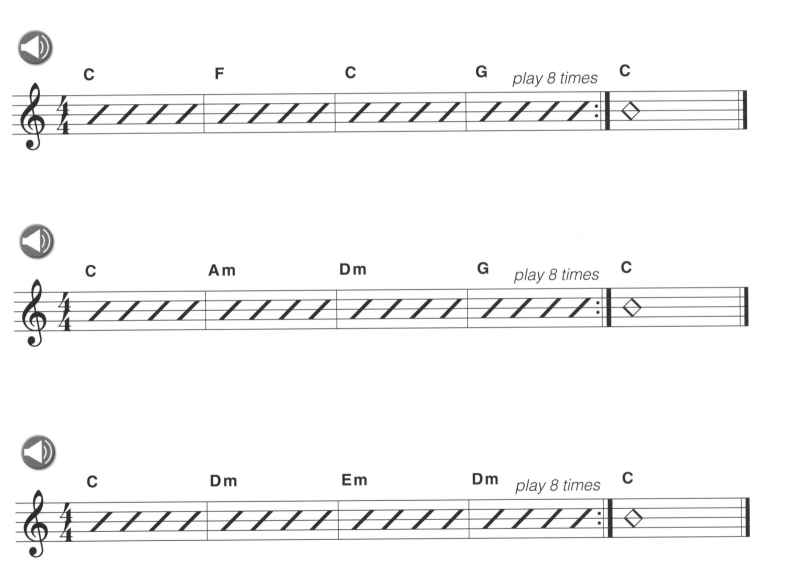

See the Reference Section at the end of this book for more information on chord construction.

G MAJOR SCALE

To build a G major scale, start with the note G and apply the major-scale step pattern. The F is sharped to complete the pattern.

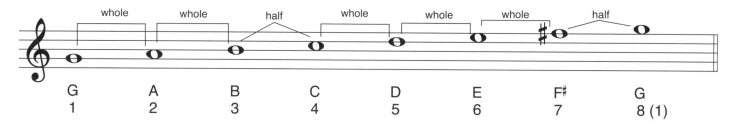

G	A	B	C	D	E	F#	G
1	2	3	4	5	6	7	8 (1)

The triads built on the notes in the G major scale are:

Practice the G major scale in first position. Remember: the key signature for G major is one sharp (F#).

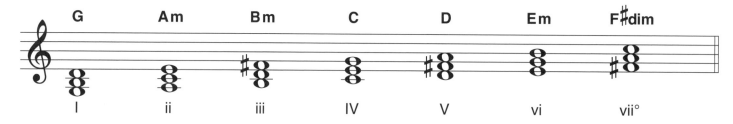

Now play a well-known melody using notes and chords from the G major scale.

THE FIRST NOEL

98

D MAJOR SCALE

To build a D major scale, start with the note D and apply the major-scale step pattern.

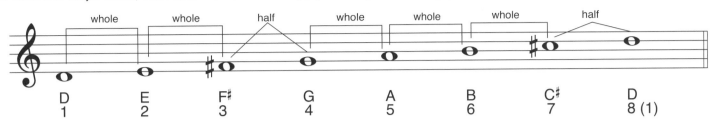

The triads built on the notes in the D major scale are:

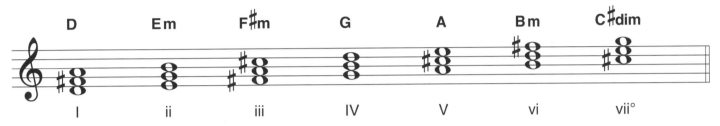

Practice the D major scale ascending and descending in first position. Remember: the key signature for D major is two sharps (F♯ and C♯).

RIFF IN D

The major scale step pattern can be applied to any root note to create any major scale. If you start on E, you will have an E major scale. If you start on F, you will have an F major scale. If you start on F♯, you will have an F♯ major scale, and so on.

SIXTEENTH NOTES

The **sixteenth note** has a solid oval head with a stem and either two flags or two beams. It lasts half as long as the eighth note.

The following chart shows the relationship of sixteenth notes to all the rhythmic values you have learned.

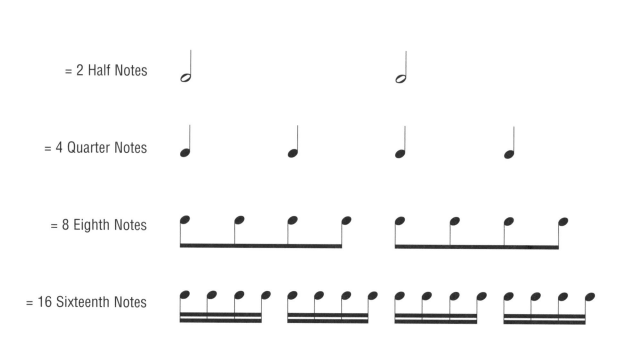

Since there are four sixteenth notes in one quarter note beat, count them by adding the syllables "e" and "a" (pronounced "uh"). The counting would be:

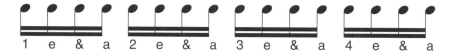

Practice the following sixteenth note exercises. Begin playing them slowly and accurately, then increase the tempo. Tap your foot on each beat of the measure.

$\frac{2}{4}$ TIME

In $\frac{2}{4}$ time there are two beats per measure and the quarter note gets one beat.

ARKANSAS TRAVELER

Fiddle Tune

SLOW/FAST

EXOTIC ROCK

13

FREEDOM ROCK

14

EINE KLEINE NACHTMUSIK
(A Little Night Music)

Mozart

15

DOTTED EIGHTH NOTES

Like the other dotted notes you've played, the dot after an eighth note increases the value of the note by one-half.

Since the dotted eighth receives only a part of a beat in $\frac{4}{4}$, $\frac{3}{4}$, or $\frac{2}{4}$ time, a sixteenth is added to it to complete the beat.

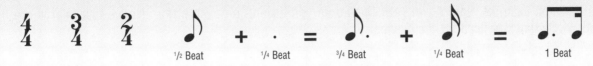

An easy way to learn a dotted eighth is to think of it as three tied sixteenth notes. This will help you play the rhythm more accurately. Practice the following exercise until you can play the subdivision of the beat easily.

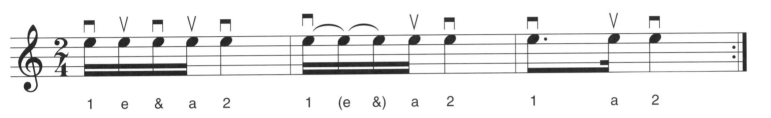

TRAMP, TRAMP, TRAMP

THE CHROMATIC SCALE

The **chromatic scale** is made up entirely of half-steps; therefore, it will use every available fret on the fretboard. If you play every fret on a given string from the open note to the twelfth fret, you will be playing a one-octave chromatic scale.

When playing the next example, hold down your fingers as you ascend on each string. Notice that sharps are used for the ascending scale while flats are used for the descent.

The diagram at the right shows all of the notes within the first twelve frets of the guitar fingerboard. Practicing the chromatic exercises below each day will greatly increase your finger dexterity and accuracy.

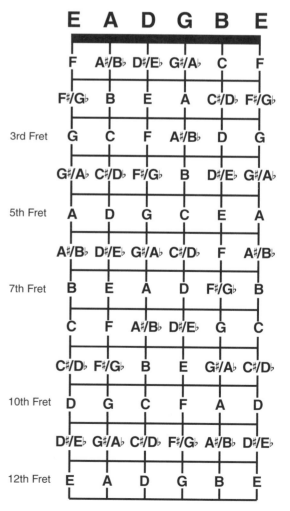

CUT TIME

Common Time 𝄴 is another way of writing $\frac{4}{4}$. Another way of writing $\frac{2}{2}$ time (two beats per measure and the half note gets one beat) is 𝄵 **cut time.**

THE ENTERTAINER

Scott Joplin

Play the next piece twice and gradually speed up.

IN THE HALL OF THE MOUNTAIN KING

E. Grieg

ESTUDIO

SLOW/FAST

ST. LOUIS BLUES

W.C. Handy

BARRE CHORDS

Barre chords are chords in which two or more strings are depressed using the same finger. Most barre chords cover five or six strings and contain no open strings. The fingering shapes are movable and can be shifted up or down the neck to different positions to produce other chords of the same quality.

E-TYPE BARRE CHORD

One of the most useful movable barre chords is the one based on the open E chord. The root note of this E shape is on the sixth string. Therefore, this shape will be used to play major chords up and down the sixth string.

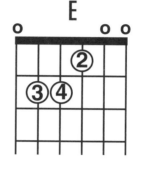

Follow these steps to form the E-type barre chord.

    1. Play an open E chord, but use your 2nd, 3rd, and 4th fingers.

    2. Slide this chord shape up one fret, and add your 1st finger across the 1st fret, forming a barre.

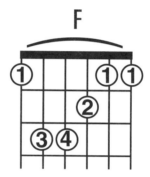

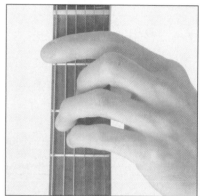

Strum all six strings to play your first barre chord. Make sure each string rings out clearly. Strike each note one at a time to test for clarity.

This particular barre chord is F major because its root is F on the sixth string. You can apply this same shape to any root note along the sixth string:

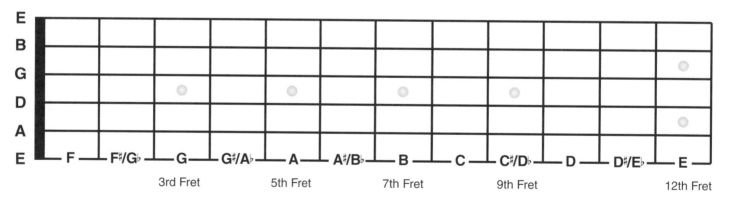

Now try the following barre chord exercise to get used to the feel of the movable shape.

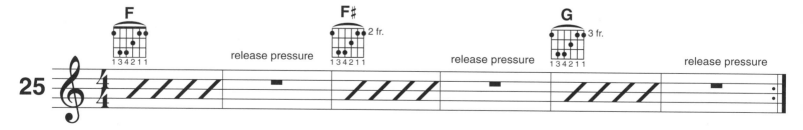

Once you are familiar with the basic feel and movement of the E-type major barre chord, it is easy to adapt this shape to form minor, seventh, and minor seventh barre chords.

If you subtract your 2nd finger from the major barre chord, you have a minor barre chord. If you subtract your 4th finger from the major barre chord, you have a seventh barre chord. If you subtract your 2nd and 4th fingers from the major barre chord, you have a minor seventh barre chord. Study the photos and diagrams below.

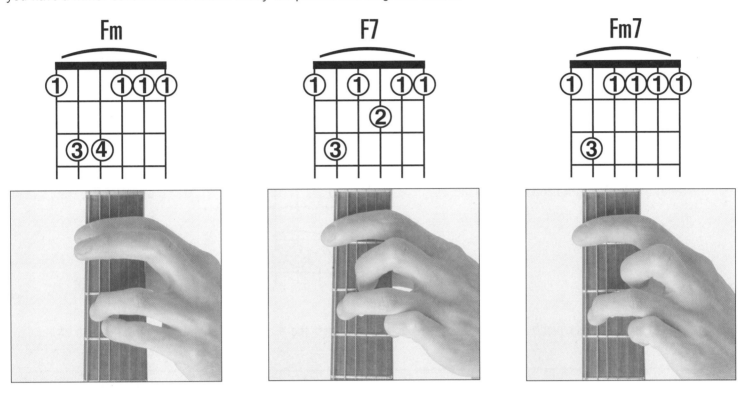

Try using these new barre chords in the examples below.

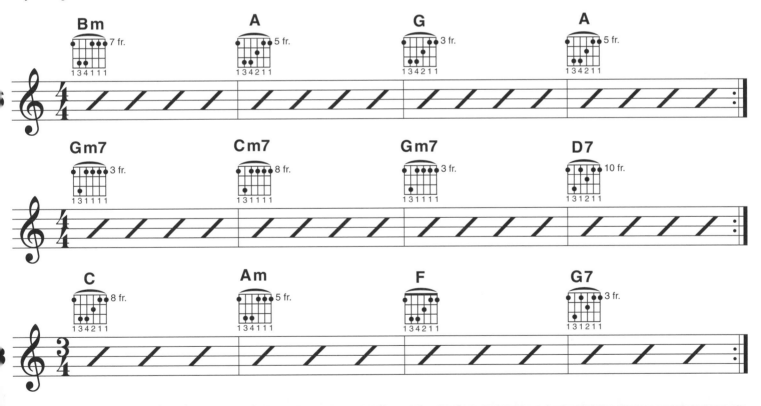

BARRE CHORD TIPS

Having difficulty at first in playing barre chords is normal. Here are some tips to help you:
- Instead of holding your first finger totally flat, rotate it a little onto its side nearest the thumb.
- Place your left thumb dirctly behind the first-finger barre for additional support.
- Move your elbow of your left arm in close to your body, even to the point that it's touching your body at the waist.

A-TYPE BARRE CHORD

The open A chord can also be converted to a barre chord. This shape will have its root on the fifth string. Follow these steps:

1. Play an open A chord, but use your 3rd finger to barre across strings 2-4.

2. Slide this chord shape up one fret, and add your 1st finger across the 1st fret, forming a barre.

The new B♭ barre chord can be tricky at first. If you are having trouble elevating the middle knuckle of your 3rd finger, you may want to avoid playing the first string (either by not striking it with the right hand or by muting it).

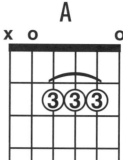

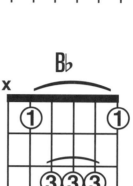

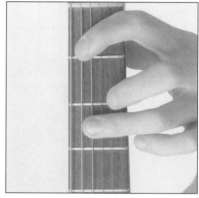

Practice the A-type major barre chord up and down the neck. Remember: the root of this shape lies along the fifth string.

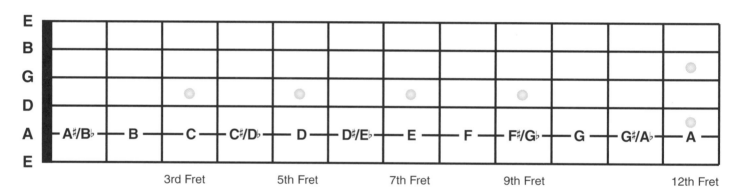

Now, use the major barre chord shape you just learned to play the following exercises.

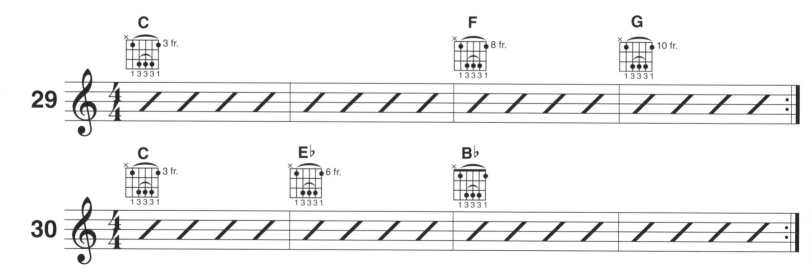

Playing barre chords on a electric guitar is easier than playing them on an acoustic guitar. This is because the **string gauges** (the thickness of the strings) are lighter on an electric guitar and the **action** (distance of the strings to the fretboard) is lower than on an acoustic.

The three barre chord shapes below are derived from the A-type major barre chord you just learned.

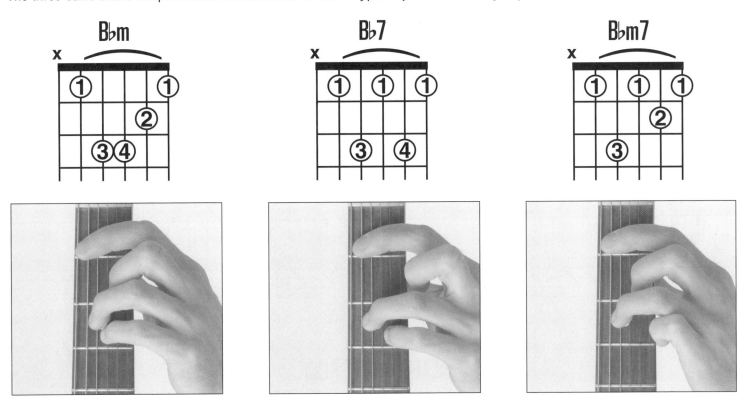

The following exercises combine the four A-type barre chords.

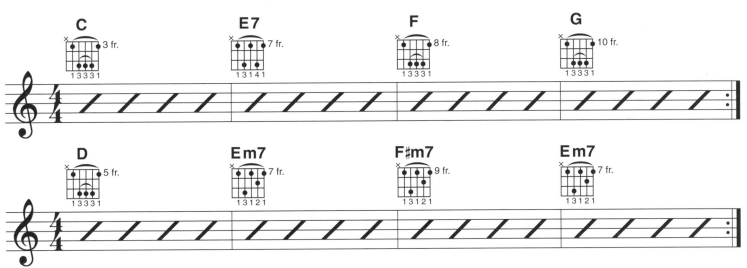

Sometimes you will see barre chords written in standard notation and tablature.

CLASSIC ROCK

Now try some songs which use E-type and A-type barre chords.

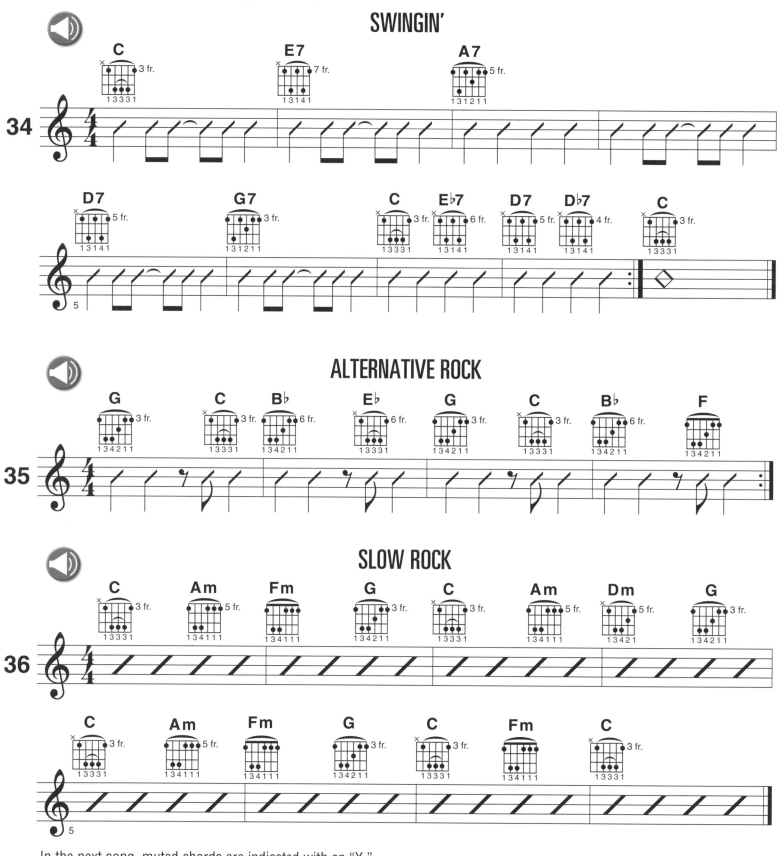

In the next song, muted chords are indicated with an "X."

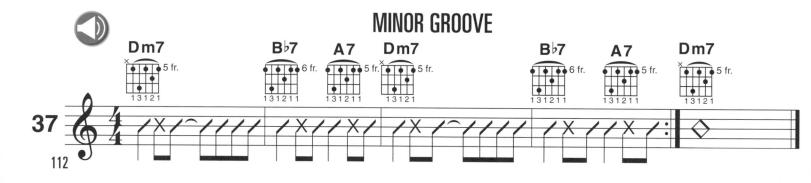

Some songs contain both barre chords and open chords.

JAZZY

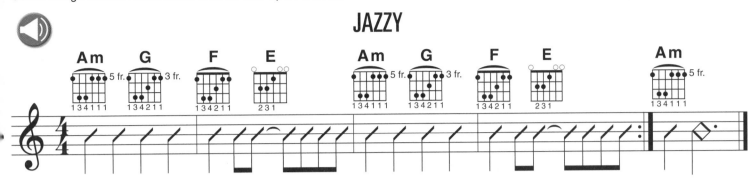

The next song introduces a new A-type barre chord: the major seventh chord. Also featured is a syncopated strum pattern that is common to Latin jazz.

BOSSA NOVA

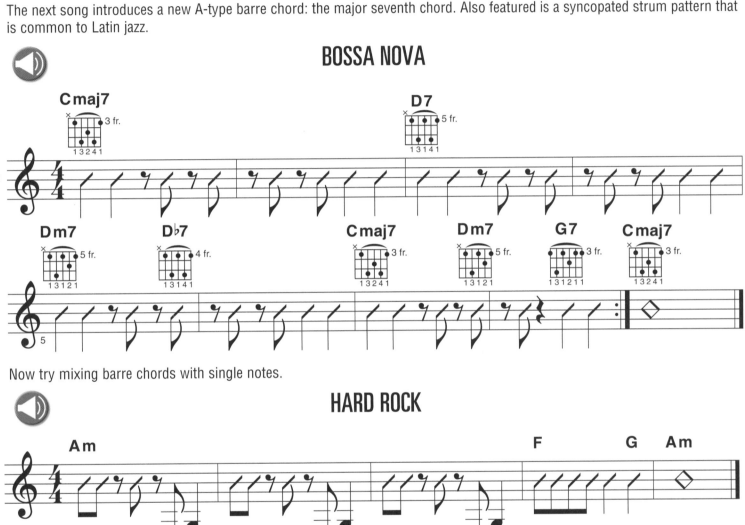

Now try mixing barre chords with single notes.

HARD ROCK

BARRE EXAM

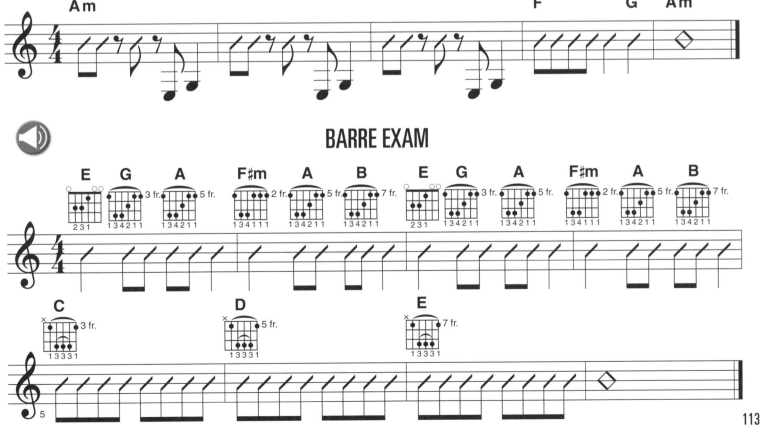

TRAVIS PICKING

Travis picking, named after country guitarist Merle Travis, is one of the most popular fingerstyle techniques. The style features two main characteristics:

- The thumb alternates between two bass strings, either on beats 1 and 3 or in steady quarter notes.
- The fingers pluck the higher strings, usually between the bass notes (on the off-beats).

The result is a driving, rhythmic feel that you can use for a variety of settings from ragtime to blues and beyond.

Practice each of the two main Travis picking patterns below. Notice the difference in the use of the thumb bass notes. Count the rhythms aloud as you play.

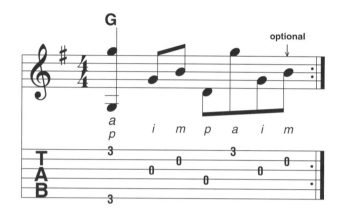 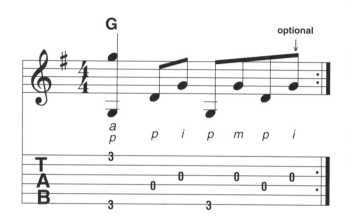

Now practice Travis picking on the following chord progressions. Start by playing one chord at a time; then gradually try moving from chord to chord. Optional bass notes are shown in parentheses.

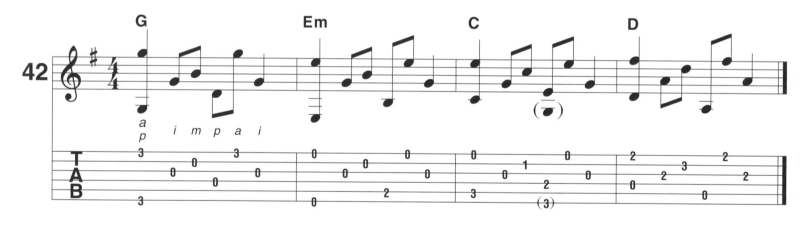

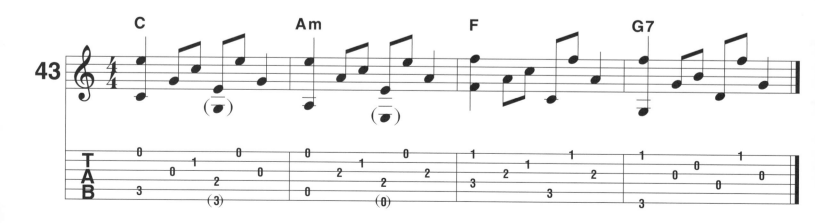

SOMETIMES I FEEL LIKE A MOTHERLESS CHILD

African American Traditional

2. Sometimes I feel like I got no home.
   Sometimes I feel like I got no home.
   Sometimes I feel like I got no home,
   a long way from home, a long way from home.

3. Sometimes I feel like a feather in the air.
   Sometimes I feel like a feather in the air.
   Sometimes I feel like a feather in the air,
   a long way from home, a long way from home.

African American Traditional

SLOW/FAST

2. When I die, Lord, bury me deep
down at the end of old Chestnut Street.
So I can hear old Number Nine
as she comes rollin' down the line.

3. When I'm dead and in my grave,
no more good times will I crave.
Place a stone at my head and feet,
and tell them that I've gone to sleep.

DROP D TUNING

Alternate tunings are tunings other than the standard (low to high) E–A–D–G–B–E tuning. By using alternate tunings, you can achieve new, exciting sounds that are impossible to attain in standard tuning. Alternate tunings may also enable you to play licks or chords that are difficult to finger in standard tuning. Artists as diverse as Joni Mitchell, Robert Johnson, the Rolling Stones, and Nirvana make use of alternate tunings.

Drop D Tuning is the alternate tuning that is closest to standard tuning—you retune only the sixth string. To get into this tuning, lower (drop) your sixth string until it sounds an octave lower than your fourth string.

This tuning enables you to play a D (or Dm) chord with a low D as a root on the sixth string, giving you a full, rich sound.

POP/ROCK

An advantage of drop D tuning is that you can play low power chords on the bottom two strings as two-string barres, as shown in the next example.

GRUNGE

Finally, try mixing Travis Picking with drop D tuning.

FOLK/ROCK

MOVABLE SCALES

You already know how to play scales in first position. To become a skillful soloist and proficient all-around guitarist, you must learn to play scales anywhere on the fingerboard.

The concept of movable scales is similar to that of power chords and barre chords. For each scale you will learn two movable patterns, one with its tonic on the sixth string and another with its tonic on the fifth string. By using these tonics as a point of reference, you can move the scales up and down the neck to accommodate any key. Simply match one of the tonics to its respective note on the fingerboard, and the rest of the pattern follows accordingly.

THE MAJOR SCALE

Study the following movable major scale patterns. Tonics are indicated with an open circle.

Tonic on Sixth String   Tonic on Fifth String

A Major Scale

D Major Scale

Use alternate picking as you practice the following major scale exercises.

G Major Scale Pattern

C Major Scale Pattern

MISS McLEOD'S REEL

Traditional

THE MINOR SCALE
Study the following movable minor scale patterns.

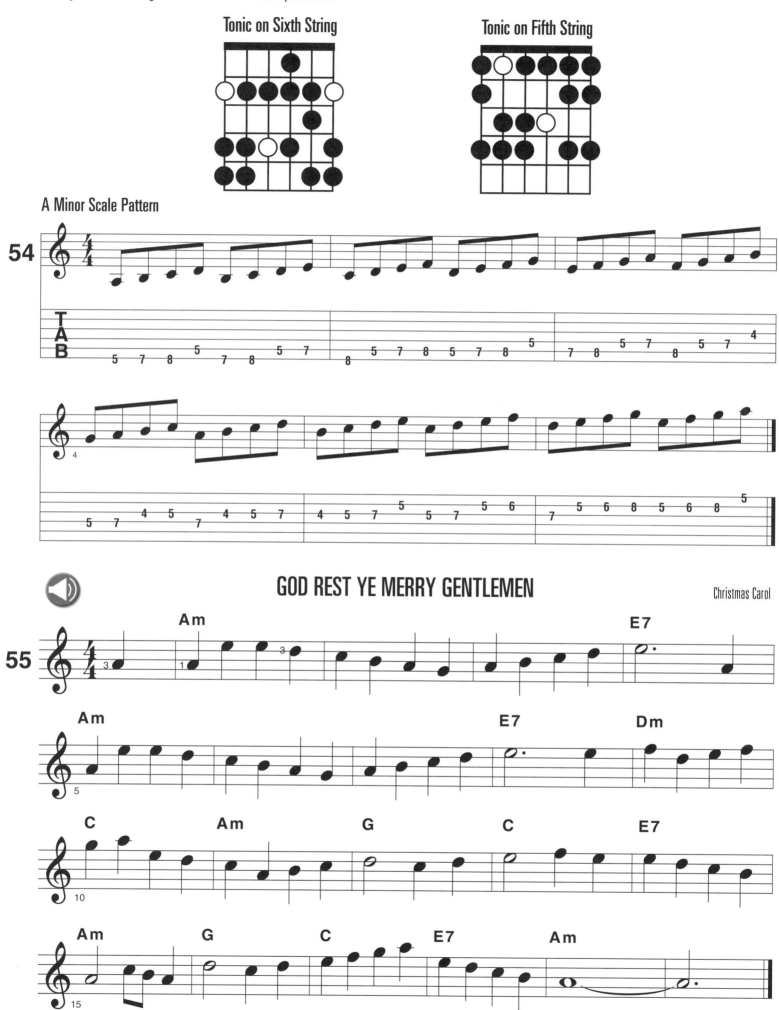

Tonic on Sixth String

Tonic on Fifth String

A Minor Scale Pattern

GOD REST YE MERRY GENTLEMEN

Christmas Carol

THE MINOR PENTATONIC SCALE

Study the following movable minor pentatonic scale patterns.

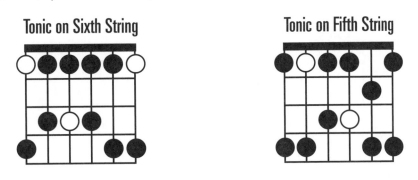

Tonic on Sixth String   **Tonic on Fifth String**

G Minor Pentatonic Riff

C Minor Pentatonic Lick

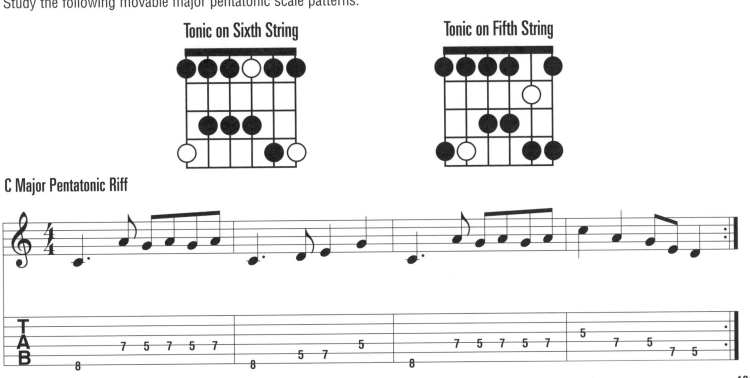

THE MAJOR PENTATONIC SCALE

Study the following movable major pentatonic scale patterns.

Tonic on Sixth String   **Tonic on Fifth String**

C Major Pentatonic Riff

FIFTH POSITION

The **fifth position** is very useful for playing songs, riffs, and licks in a higher position on the neck. Fingers 1, 2, 3, and 4 play in frets 5, 6, 7, and 8 as indicated in the diagram below.

Notice that some notes can be played in an alternate position on the fretboard. Shift your first finger down to fret notes that need to be played on the fourth fret and stretch your fourth finger to fret notes that need to be played on the ninth fret.

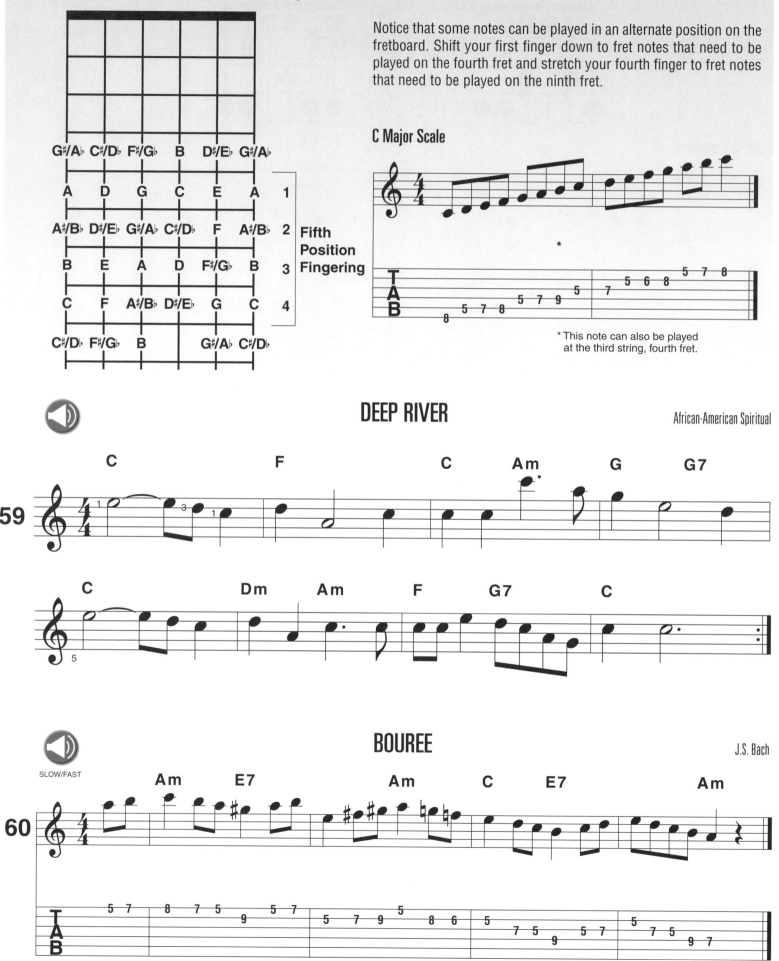

* This note can also be played at the third string, fourth fret.

DEEP RIVER

African-American Spiritual

BOUREE

J.S. Bach

SLOW/FAST

HEAVY ROCK

JAZZIN' THE BLUES

THE KEY OF F

The key signature for F has one flat. All Bs should be played one half step lower.

F Major Scale, First Position

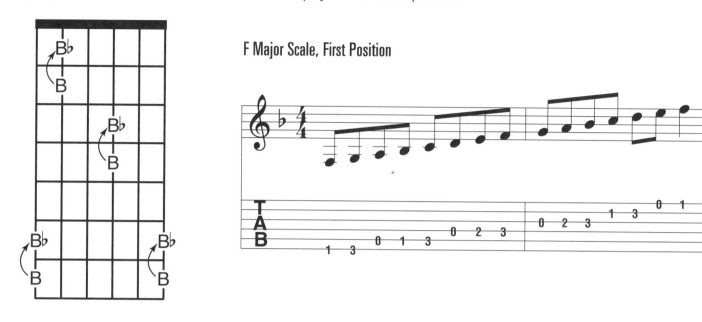

Play the melody to "Sloop John B." in fifth position; then figure out how to play the chords to the song using the barre forms you learned on pages 108-113. You may also wish to try playing the Travis picking accompaniment from pages 114-116.

SLOOP JOHN B.

Caribbean

Refer to the "Circle of Fifths" on page 134 for more on keys.

COMPOUND TIME

Until now you have played time signatures in which the quarter note received one beat (e.g, $\frac{2}{4}$, $\frac{3}{4}$, $\frac{4}{4}$). The rhythmic pulse of these time signatures is divisible by two—four sixteenth notes equal two eighth notes, two eighth notes equal one quarter note, etc. This is called **simple time**. A time signature in which the rhythmic pulse is divisible by three is called **compound time**. The most common examples of compound time are $\frac{6}{8}$ and $\frac{12}{8}$.

$\frac{6}{8}$ **TIME** In $\frac{6}{8}$ time the bottom number tells you that the eighth note gets one beat and the top number tells you that there are six beats in one measure. All note and rest values are proportionate to the eighth note.

Eighth = 1 Beat   Quarter = 2 Beats   Dotted Quarter = 3 Beats

Practice playing "I Saw Three Ships" in fifth position. Be sure to follow the count carefully.

I SAW THREE SHIPS

$\frac{12}{8}$ **TIME** The $\frac{12}{8}$ time signature is based on the same principle as $\frac{6}{8}$ time. In $\frac{12}{8}$ there are twelve beats per measure and the eighth note gets one beat.

SLOW BLUES

ARTICULATION

Articulation refers to how you play and connect notes on the guitar. If pitches and rhythms are what you play, articulation is how you play. **Slides**, **hammer-ons**, **pull-offs**, and **bends** all belong to a special category of articulations called **legato**. Legato techniques allow you to "slur" two or more notes together to create a smooth, flowing sound and help give your music flavor and expression.

THE SLIDE

The slide is played by following these steps:

- Depress the string with the left-hand finger.
- Pick the string with the right hand.
- Maintain pressure as you move your left-hand finger up or down the fretboard to the second position shown. (The second note is not picked.)

BOUNCY BLUES

POWER CHORD SLIDES

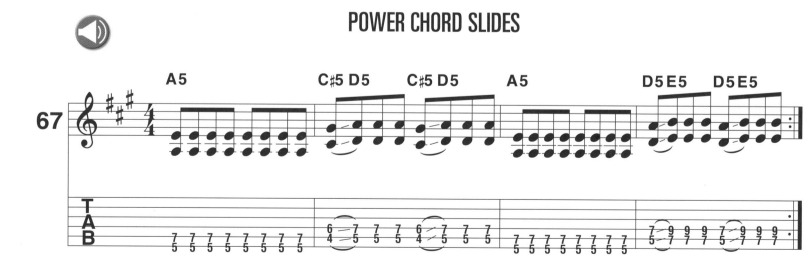

THE HAMMER-ON

The **hammer-on** is named for the action of the left-hand fingers on the fretboard. To play the hammer-on follow these steps:

- Depress the string with the left-hand finger.
- Pick the string with the right hand.
- Maintain pressure as you quickly press down onto the fret of the second (higher) note on the same string, using the initial attack to carry the tone.

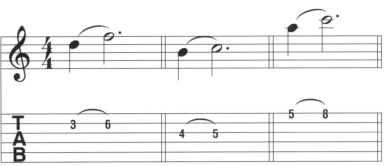

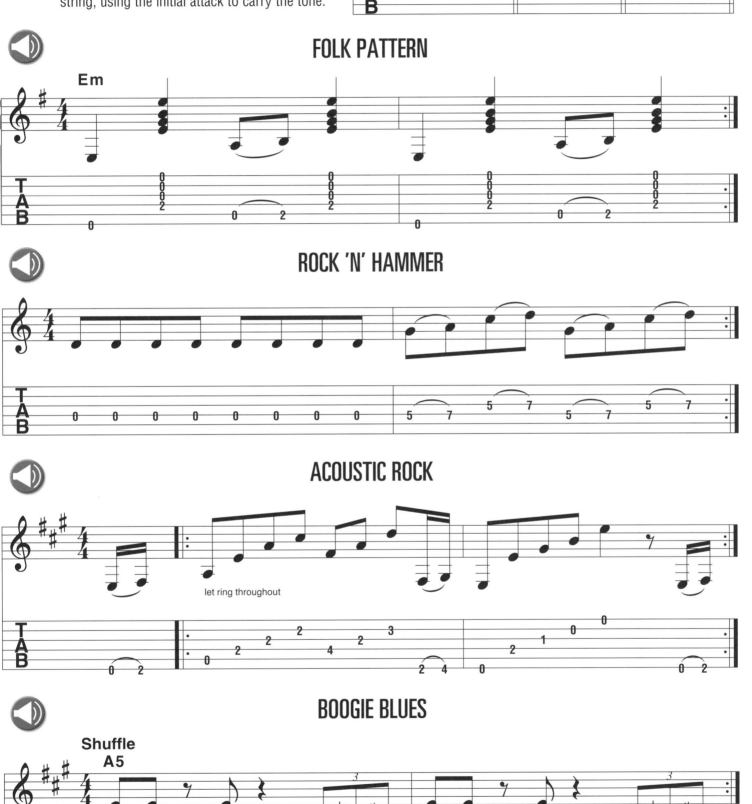

FOLK PATTERN

ROCK 'N' HAMMER

ACOUSTIC ROCK

let ring throughout

BOOGIE BLUES

Shuffle

THE PULL-OFF

The **pull-off** is the opposite of the hammer-on. To play the pull-off follow these steps:

- Depress the string with the left-hand finger.
- Pick the string with the right hand.
- Maintain pressure as you pull the left-hand finger toward the palm of your hand to sound the note behind it on the same string, using the initial attack to carry the tone.

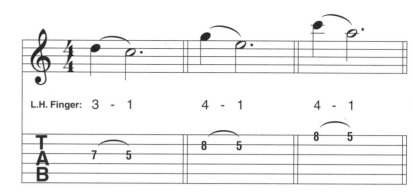

POWER PULL

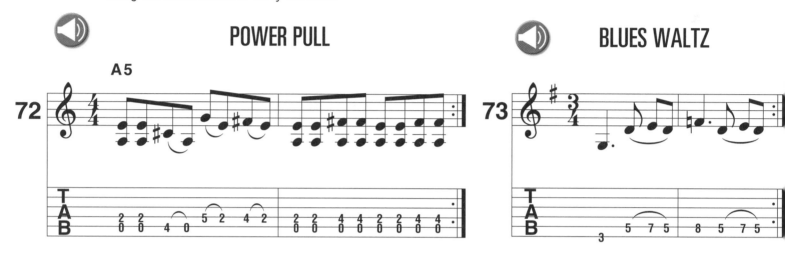

BLUES WALTZ

Hammer-ons, pull-offs, and slides are all used in the next example.

BLUEGRASS RUN

SLOW/FAST

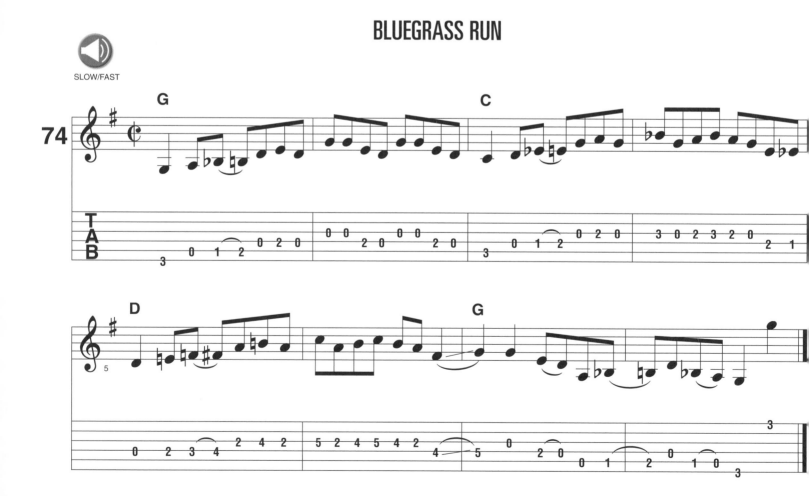

THE STRING BEND

The **string bend** produces the vocal-like sound of blues, rock, and pop guitar. To bend a string follow these steps:

- Depress the string with the left-hand 3rd finger.
- Maintain pressure as you push the string upward or pull it downward.
- Use your first and second fingers for additional support.

Bends are indicated in music by a pointed slur in standard notation and an arrow in tablature. Bending strings works best on steel-string guitars and is done most easily on the first three strings.

To the right are some characteristic bends:

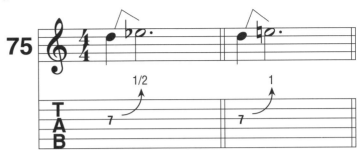

ROCK LICK

The next example contains a bend and release. Maintain pressure as you lower the bend back to its original pitch.

SWAMPY BLUES

Now try bending two strings at the same time.

DOUBLE-STOP BEND

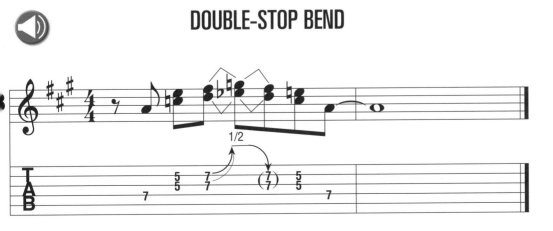

JAM SESSION

Now it is time to use the chords and scales you know to make some of your own music. This section provides ten chord progressions found in various music styles. You can either follow the chord symbols and strum along, or use the suggested scales to practice improvising. Listen to the recording and copy the solo licks; then try creating your own solos. If you don't have the recording, take turns playing rhythm and leads with friends or record your own rhythm tracks and play lead over them.

Each of the jam tracks begins with Greg Koch playing solos over the first two times through. Use these as a model for what you can play on the remaining six times through.

POP/ROCK BALLAD

Suggested scales: G major and G major pentatonic

FUNK

Suggested scale: A minor pentatonic

SMOOTH JAZZ

Suggested scales: C major and C major pentatonic

LATIN ROCK

Suggested scales: D minor and D minor pentatonic

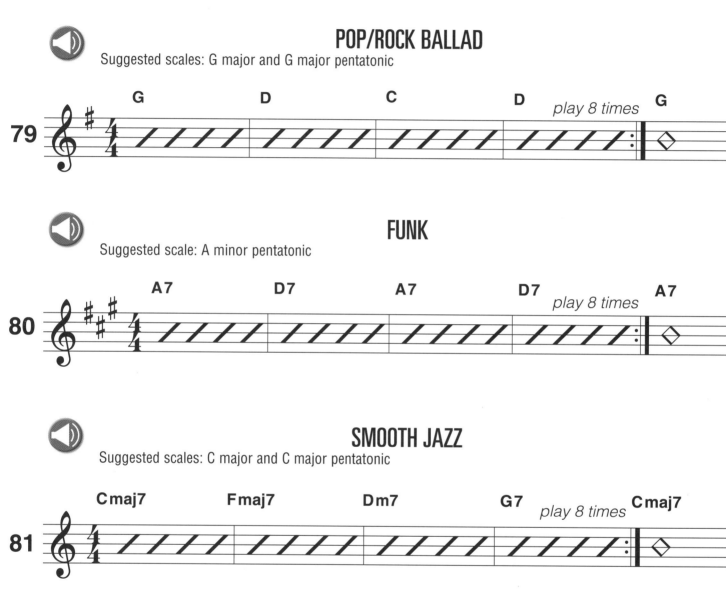

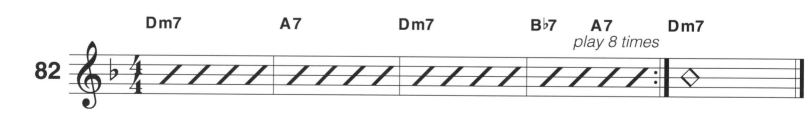

GRAND FINALE

SLOW/FAST

89

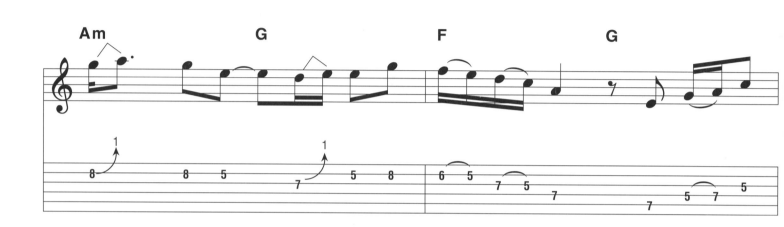

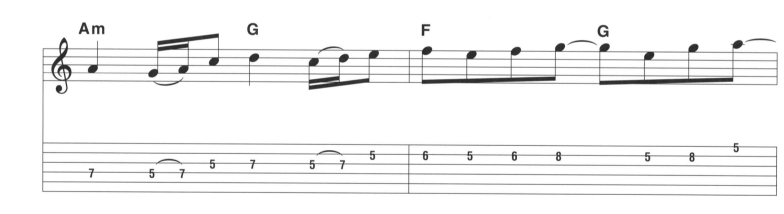

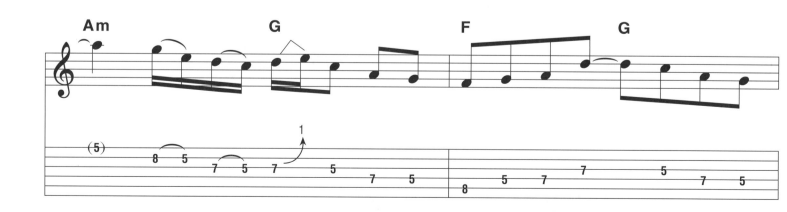

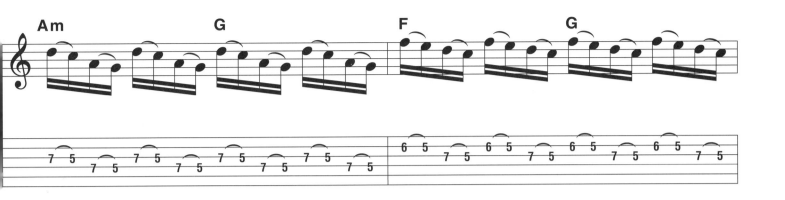

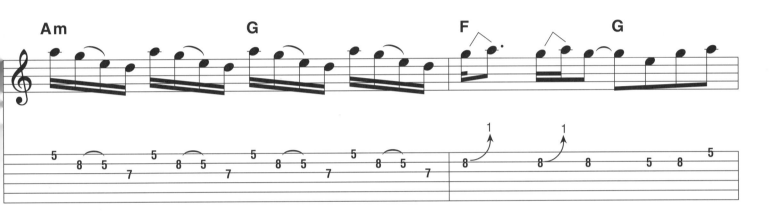

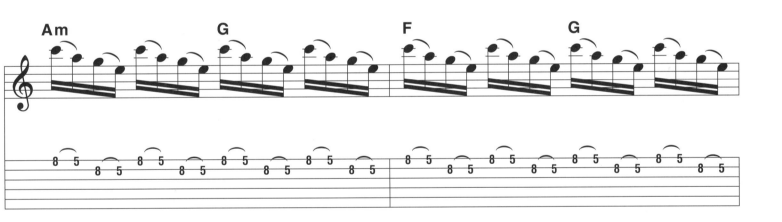

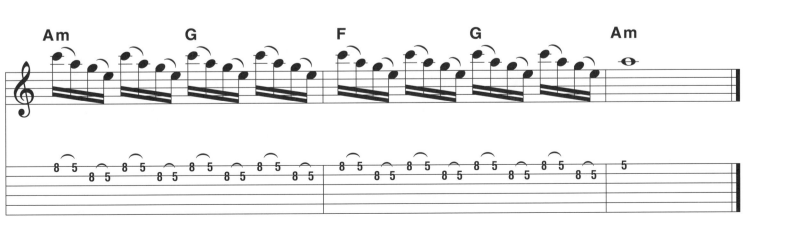

REFERENCE SECTION

CIRCLE OF FIFTHS

The **circle of fifths** is a useful tool if you want to know what chords are common within a key. Major keys line the outside of the circle; their relative minors line the inside.

Right now, the box is highlighting chords that belong to both C major and its relative A minor. To find the chords for another key, just mentally rotate the box.

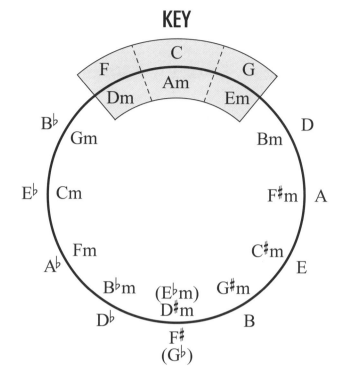

KEY

THREE-NOTE CHORD FORMS

These movable three-note shapes are easy to play and commonly used in pop, funk, and reggae styles. Pay attention to the root in each voicing; it tells you what chord you are playing.

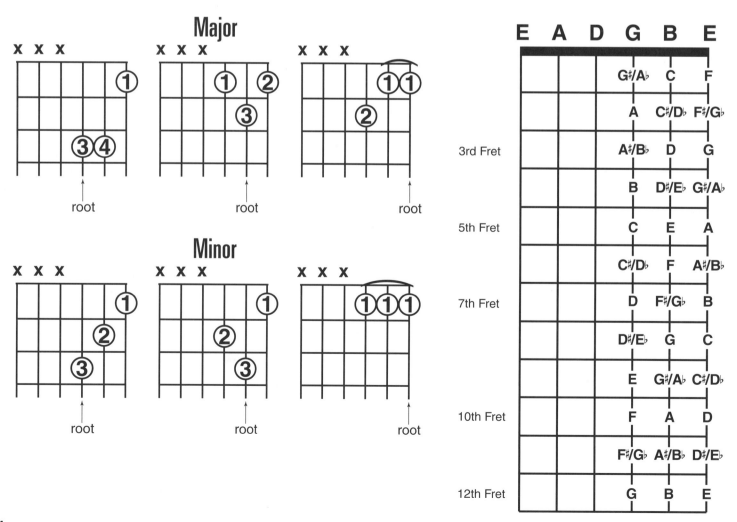

134

MISCELLANEOUS CHORDS

Below are some less common open chords which you have not learned up to this point.

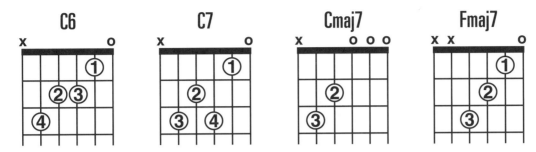

In **sus chords**, you replace the third of a chord with the fourth, as in sus4 (pronounced "suss-four") or sometimes with the second, as in sus2. The resulting sound is incomplete or unresolved but creates an interesting sound that is neither major nor minor.

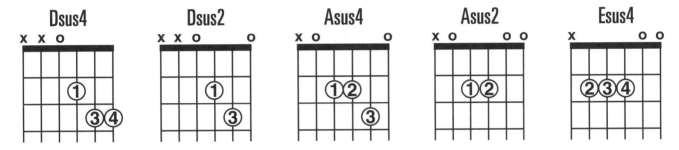

An **add chord** is simply a basic chord (such as a major chord) to which you add an extra note. If you take a C chord and add a D note to it, for example, you have a Cadd2 chord (with notes C–D–E–G). This chord is different from Csus2, which has no E.

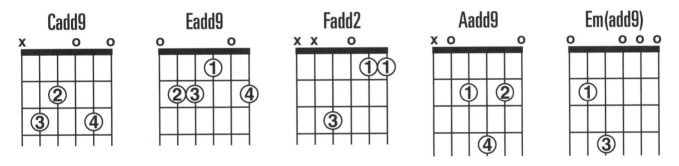

Slash chords are colorful, interesting chords that add spice and flavor to all styles of music. A slash chord is, simply, a chord with a slash (/) in its name, as in G/B (pronounced "G over B"). To the left of the slash is the chord itself; to the right of the slash is the bass note for that chord.

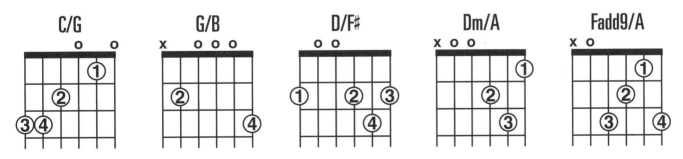

CHORD CONSTRUCTION

All chords are constructed using intervals. An **interval** is the distance between any two notes. Though there are many types of intervals, there are only five categories: major, minor, perfect, augmented, and diminished. Interestingly, the major scale contains only major and perfect intervals:

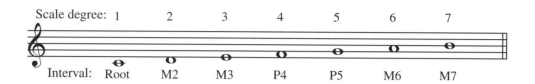

The major scale also happens to be a great starting point from which to construct chords. For example, if we start at the root (C) and add the interval of a major third (E) and a perfect fifth (G), we have constructed a C major chord.

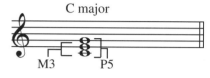

In order to construct a chord other than a major chord, at least one of the major or perfect intervals needs to be altered. For example, take the C major chord you just constructed, and lower the third degree (E) one half step. We now have a C minor chord: C-E♭-G. By lowering the major third by one half step, we create a new interval called a **minor** third.

We can further alter the chord by flatting the perfect fifth (G). The chord is now a Cdim: C-E♭-G♭. The G♭ represents a **diminished** fifth interval.

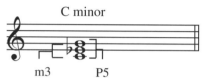

This leads us to a basic rule of thumb to help remember interval alterations:

A major interval lowered one half step is a minor interval.

A perfect interval lowered one half step is a diminished interval.

A perfect interval raised one half step is an augmented interval.

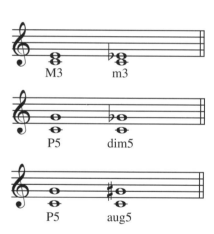

Half steps and whole steps are the building blocks of intervals; they determine an interval's quality—major, minor, etc. On the guitar, a half step is just the distance from one fret to the next. A whole step is equal to two half steps, or two frets.

Notice that we assigned a numerical value to each note in the major scale, as well as labeling the intervals. These numerical values, termed **scale degrees**, allow us to "generically" construct chords, regardless of key. For example, a major chord consists of the root (1), major third (3), and perfect fifth (5). Substitute any major scale for the C major scale above, select scale degrees 1, 3, and 5, and you will have a major chord for the scale you selected.

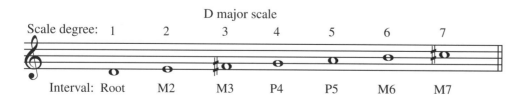

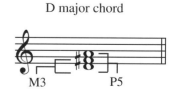

The chart below is a construction summary of 44 chord types (based on the key of C only) using the scale degree method:

CHORD TYPE	FORMULA	NOTES	CHORD NAME
major	1-3-5	C-E-G	C
fifth (power chord)	1-5	C-G	C5
suspended fourth	1-4-5	C-F-G	Csus4
suspended second	1-2-5	C-D-G	Csus2
added ninth	1-3-5-9	C-E-G-D	Cadd9
sixth	1-3-5-6	C-E-G-A	C6
sixth, added ninth	1-3-5-6-9	C-E-G-A-D	C6/9
major seventh	1-3-5-7	C-E-G-B	Cmaj7
major ninth	1-3-5-7-9	C-E-G-B-D	Cmaj9
major seventh, sharp eleventh	1-3-5-7-♯11	C-E-G-B-F♯	Cmaj7♯11
major thirteenth	1-3-5-7-9-13	C-E-G-B-D-A	Cmaj13
minor	1-♭3-5	C-E♭-G	Cm
minor, added ninth	1-♭3-5-9	C-E♭-G-D	Cm(add9)
minor sixth	1-♭3-5-6	C-E♭-G-A	Cm6
minor, flat sixth	1-♭3-5-♭6	C-E♭-G-A♭	Cm♭6
minor sixth, added ninth	1-♭3-5-6-9	C-E♭-G-A-D	Cm6/9
minor seventh	1-♭3-5-♭7	C-E♭-G-B♭	Cm7
minor seventh, flat fifth	1-♭3-♭5-♭7	C-E♭-G♭-B♭	Cm7♭5
minor, major seventh	1-♭3-5-7	C-E♭-G-B	Cm(maj7)
minor ninth	1-♭3-5-♭7-9	C-E♭-G-B♭-D	Cm9
minor ninth, flat fifth	1-♭3-♭5-♭7-9	C-E♭-G♭-B♭-D	Cm9♭5
minor ninth, major seventh	1-♭3-5-7-9	C-E♭-G-B-D	Cm9(maj7)
minor eleventh	1-♭3-5-♭7-9-11	C-E♭-G-B♭-D-F	Cm11
minor thirteenth	1-♭3-5-♭7-9-11-13	C-E♭-G-B♭-D-F-A	Cm13
dominant seventh	1-3-5-♭7	C-E-G-B♭	C7
seventh, suspended fourth	1-4-5-♭7	C-F-G-B♭	C7sus4
seventh, flat fifth	1-3-♭5-♭7	C-E-G♭-B♭	C7♭5
ninth	1-3-5-♭7-9	C-E-G-B♭-D	C9
ninth, suspended fourth	1-4-5-♭7-9	C-F-G-B♭-D	C9sus4
ninth, flat fifth	1-3-♭5-♭7-9	C-E-G♭-B♭-D	C9♭5
seventh, flat ninth	1-3-5-♭7-♭9	C-E-G-B♭-D♭	C7♭9
seventh, sharp ninth	1-3-5-♭7-♯9	C-E-G-B♭-D♯	C7♯9
seventh, flat fifth, sharp ninth	1-3-♭5-♭7-♯9	C-E-G♭-B♭-D♯	C7♭5(♯9)
eleventh	1-5-♭7-9-11	C-G-B♭-D-F	C11
seventh, sharp eleventh	1-3-5-♭7-♯11	C-E-G-B♭-F♯	C7♯11
thirteenth	1-3-5-♭7-9-13	C-E-G-B♭-D-A	C13
thirteenth, suspended fourth	1-4-5-♭7-9-13	C-F-G-B♭-D-A	C13sus4
augmented	1-3-♯5	C-E-G♯	Caug
seventh, sharp fifth	1-3-♯5-♭7	C-E-G♯-B♭	Caug7
ninth, sharp fifth	1-3-♯5-♭7-9	C-E-G♯-B♭-D	Caug9
seventh, sharp fifth, flat ninth	1-3-♯5-♭7-♭9	C-E-G♯-B♭-D♭	Caug7♭9
seventh, sharp fifth, sharp ninth	1-3-♯5-♭7-♯9	C-E-G♯-B♭-D♯	Caug7♯9
diminished	1-♭3-♭5	C-E♭-G♭	Cdim
diminished seventh	1-♭3-♭5-♭♭7	C-E♭-G♭-B♭♭	Cdim7

Triads

The most basic chords are called triads. A **triad** is a chord that is made up of only three notes. For example, a simple G major chord is a triad consisting of the notes G, B, and D. There are several types of triads, including major, minor, diminished, augmented, and suspended. All of these chords are constructed by simply altering the relationships between the root note and the intervals.

Sevenths

To create more interesting harmony, you can take the familiar triad and add another interval: the seventh. **Seventh chords** are comprised of four notes: the three notes of the triad plus a major or minor seventh interval. For example, if you use the G major triad (G-B-D) and add a major seventh interval (F#), the Gmaj7 chord is formed. Likewise, if you substitute the minor seventh interval (F) for the F#, you have a new seventh chord, the G7. This is also known as a dominant seventh chord, popularly used in blues and jazz music. As with the triads, seventh chords come in many types, including major, minor, diminished, augmented, suspended, and others.

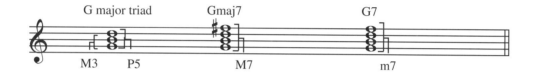

Extended chords

Extended chords are those that include notes beyond the seventh scale degree. These chords have a rich, complex harmony that is very common in jazz music. These include ninths, elevenths, and thirteenth chords. For example, if you take a Gmaj7 chord and add a major ninth interval (A), you get a Gmaj9 chord (G-B-D-F#-A). You can then add an additional interval, a major thirteenth (E), to form a Gmaj13 chord (G-B-D-F#-A-E). Note that the interval of a major eleventh is omitted. This is because the major eleventh sonically conflicts with the major third interval, creating a dissonance.

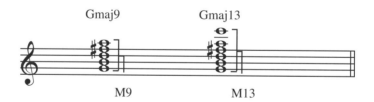

By the way, you may have noticed that these last two chords, Gmaj9 and Gmaj13, contain five and six notes, respectively; however, you only have four fingers in the left hand! Since the use of a barre chord or open-string chord is not always possible, you often need to choose the four notes of the chord that are most important to play. Below are two examples to demonstrate these chord "trimmings."

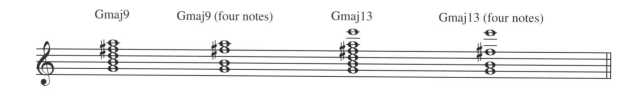

Generally speaking, the root, third, and seventh are the most crucial notes to include in an extended chord, along with the uppermost extension (ninth, thirteenth, etc.).

Inversions & Voicings

This brings us to our last topic. Though a typical chord might consist of only three or four notes—a C triad, for example, consists of just a root, third, and fifth; a G7 chord consists of a root, third, fifth, and seventh—these notes do not necessarily have to appear in that same order, from bottom to top, in the actual chords you play. Inversions are produced when you rearrange the notes of a chord:

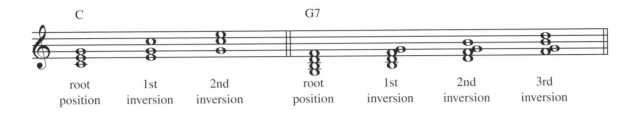

| root position | 1st inversion | 2nd inversion | root position | 1st inversion | 2nd inversion | 3rd inversion |

Practically speaking, on the guitar, notes of a chord are often inverted (rearranged), doubled (used more than once), and even omitted to create different voicings. Each voicing is unique and yet similar—kind of like different shades of the same color.

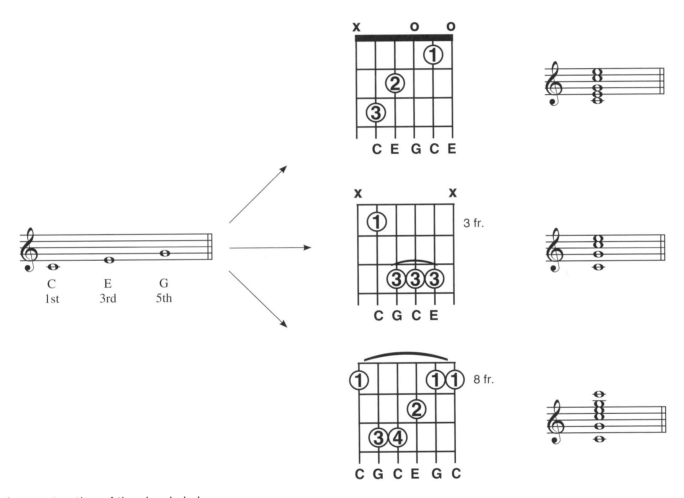

Study the construction of the chords below.

A major scale: A-B-C♯-D-E-F♯-G♯

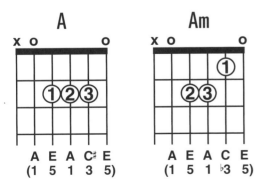

D major scale: D-E-F♯-G-A-B-C♯

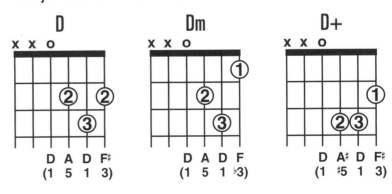

GEAR

Following are some basic guidelines to consider when choosing electric guitar equipment.

Guitars

There are three general types of electric guitars: solidbody, hollowbody, and semi-hollowbody. The **solidbody guitar** is associated most with rock, blues, country, and soul. The most popular models include the Fender Stratocaster, Gibson Les Paul, Paul Reed Smith, Fender Telecaster, Gibson SG, and Ibanez RG. The solidbody guitar is typically heavier than others. Its density permits more sustain and makes it better suited for high-volume playing. The **hollowbody guitar** is the choice of most jazz guitarists. It is distinguished by its arched top and back, f-shaped sound holes, and deep sides. The most popular models include the Gibson ES-175, Gibson L-5, Gibson Super 400, Epiphone Emperor, Heritage Eagle, Guild Manhattan, and various makes by D'Angelico, D'Aquisto, and Benedetto. The tone of the hollowbody guitar is more subdued than that of the solidbody, and its basic design makes it better suited for low to mid volume playing. The **semi-hollowbody guitar** has a thin, semi-hollow body with a solid wooden strip in the center. The most popular models include the Gibson ES-355, Gibson ES-345, Guild Starfire IV, Heritage H-535, and Epiphone Sheraton. It is most commonly used by blues, jazz-rock, and rock guitarists, and is known for providing the best of both worlds in terms of tone: more crisp than a hollowbody and more mellow than a solidbody.

The playability of various electric guitars is subjective. In trying to decide on a prospective guitar, consider the neck radius, scale length, neck material (rosewood, maple, ebony), string gauge, and fret size.

Amps

There are two general types of amps: tube and solid-state. **Tube amps** are so-named because they are powered by and get their tonal characteristics from vacuum tubes. They produce a warm, smooth clean tone and, when the volume is turned up, a natural distortion. They are favored by most blues, jazz, country, and roots-rock guitarists. **Solid-state amps** use transistors for power and tone. They are typically more reliable and versatile than tube amps and have come a long way in recent years in terms of being able to produce a warm tone. In the late 1990s, digital modeling technology has enabled solid-state amps to access an assortment of classic tube amp tones and a myriad of effects. Solid-state amps are preferred by most modern rock guitarists, but are also widely used for playing all musical styles.

Effects

Effects are devices that plug in between your guitar and amp and enable you to alter your signal in a variety of ways. They are available as individual units, called **foot pedals**, or as an all-in-one box, called a **multi-effects processor**. Following is a list of the most popular effects:

Distortion	Simulates the sound of a guitar signal driven too hard for the amp; the effect can produce anything from a bright, fuzzy tone to a thick, dirty tone.
Chorus	Simulates the sound of two guitars playing at once; the effect can produce anything from a lush, chiming sound to a warbled, fluttering sound.
Delay or Echo	Simulates the repetition of sound; the effect can add depth to your tone by producing anything from a short, "slap back" delay to a longer, ambient looping sound.
Reverb	Simulates the natural echo produced in various rooms; the effect can produce anything from a washy, distant-sounding ambiance to a live, airy sound.
Wah-Wah Pedal	Produces a sweeping, vocal-like tone by rocking the treble back and forth.

Pickups

There are two general types of pickups: humbucking (double-coil) and single-coil. **Humbucking pickups** produce a dark, mellow sound when playing with a clean tone and a thick, heavy tone when playing with a distorted tone. **Single-coil pickups** produce a glassy, percussive sound when playing with a clean tone and an aggressive, biting tone when playing with a distorted tone.

DEFINITIONS FOR SPECIAL GUITAR NOTATION

HALF-STEP BEND: Strike the note and bend up 1/2 step.

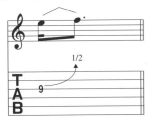

WHOLE-STEP BEND: Strike the note and bend up one step.

GRACE NOTE BEND: Strike the note and immediately bend up as indicated.

SLIGHT (MICROTONE) BEND: Strike the note and bend up 1/4 step.

BEND AND RELEASE: Strike the note and bend up as indicated, then release back to the original note. Only the first note is struck.

PRE-BEND: Bend the note as indicated, then strike it.

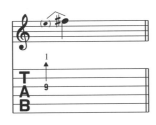

PRE-BEND AND RELEASE: Bend the note as indicated. Strike it and release the bend back to the original note.

UNISON BEND: Strike the two notes simultaneously and bend the lower note up to the pitch of the higher.

VIBRATO: The string is vibrated by rapidly bending and releasing the note with the fretting hand.

WIDE VIBRATO: The pitch is varied to a greater degree by vibrating with the fretting hand.

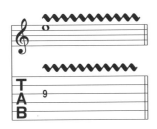

HAMMER-ON: Strike the first (lower) note with one finger, then sound the higher note (on the same string) with another finger by fretting it without picking.

PULL-OFF: Place both fingers on the notes to be sounded. Strike the first note and without picking, pull the finger off to sound the second (lower) note.

LEGATO SLIDE: Strike the first note and then slide the same fret-hand finger up or down to the second note. The second note is not struck.

SHIFT SLIDE: Same as legato slide, except the second note is struck.

TRILL: Very rapidly alternate between the notes indicated by continuously hammering on and pulling off.

TAPPING: Hammer ("tap") the fret indicated with the pick-hand index or middle finger and pull off to the note fretted by the fret hand.

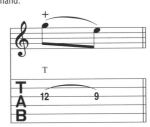

NATURAL HARMONIC: Strike the note while the fret-hand lightly touches the string directly over the fret indicated.

PINCH HARMONIC: The note is fretted normally and a harmonic is produced by adding the edge of the thumb or the tip of the index finger of the pick hand to the normal pick attack.

ARPEGGIATE: Play the notes of the chord indicated by quickly rolling them from bottom to top.

PICK SCRAPE: The edge of the pick is rubbed down (or up) the string, producing a scratchy sound.

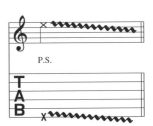

MUFFLED STRINGS: A percussive sound is produced by laying the fret hand across the string(s) without depressing, and striking them with the pick hand.

PALM MUTING: The note is partially muted by the pick hand lightly touching the string(s) just before the bridge.

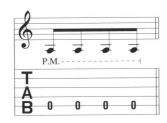

RAKE: Drag the pick across the strings indicated with a single motion.

TREMOLO PICKING: The note is picked as rapidly and continuously as possible.

HAL LEONARD GUITAR METHOD

by Will Schm[...]
and Greg Ko[...]

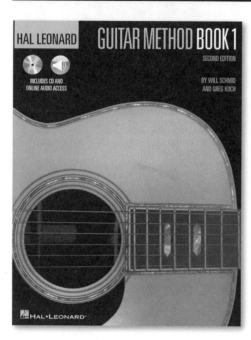

HAL LEONARD GUITAR METHOD BOOK 1
SECOND EDITION

INCLUDES CD AND
ONLINE AUDIO ACCESS

BY WILL SCHMID
AND GREG KOCH

THE HAL LEONARD GUITAR METHOD is designed for anyone just learning to play acoustic or electric guitar. It is based on [...] of teaching guitar students of all ages, and it also reflects some of the best guitar teaching ideas from around the world. [...] comprehensive method includes: A learning sequence carefully paced with clear instructions; popular songs which increas[...] incentive to learn to play; versatility – can be used as self-instruction or with a teacher; audio accompaniments so that stud[...] have fun and sound great while practicing.

BOOK 1
00699010	Book	$8.99
00699027	Book with audio on CD & Online	$12.99
00155480	Deluxe Beginner Pack (Book/DVD/CD/Online Audio & Video/Poster)	$19.99

BOOK 2
00699020	Book	$8.99
00697313	Book/CD Pack	$12.99

BOOK 3
00699030	Book	$8.99
00697316	Book/Online Audio	$12.99

COMPOSITE
Books 1, 2, and 3 bound together in an easy-to-u[...] spiral binding.
00699040	Books Only	$16[...]
00697342	Book/Online Audio	$24[...]

DVD
FOR THE BEGINNING ELECTRIC OR ACOUSTIC GUITARIST
00697318	DVD	$19[...]
00697341	Book/CD Pack and DVD	$24[...]

GUITAR FOR KIDS
A BEGINNER'S GUIDE WITH STEP-BY-STEP INSTRUCTION FOR ACOUSTIC AND ELECTRIC GUITAR
by Bob Morris and Jeff Schroedl
00865003	Book 1 – Book/Online Audio	$12[...]
00697402	Songbook Book/Online Audio	$9[...]
00128437	Book 2 – Book/Online Audio	$12[...]

SONGBOOKS

EASY POP MELODIES
00697281	Book	$6.99
00697440	Book/Online Audio	$14.99

MORE EASY POP MELODIES
00697280	Book	$6.99
00697269	Book/Online Audio	$14.99

EVEN MORE EASY POP MELODIES
00699154	Book	$6.99
00697439	Book/Online Audio	$14.99

EASY POP RHYTHMS
00697336	Book	$7.99
00697441	Book/Online Audio	$14.99

MORE EASY POP RHYTHMS
00697338	Book	$7.99
00697322	Book/Online Audio	$14.99

EVEN MORE EASY POP RHYTHMS
00697340	Book	$7.99
00697323	Book/Online Audio	$14.99

EASY SOLO GUITAR PIECES
00110407	Book	$9.99

EASY POP CHRISTMAS MELODIES
00697417	Book	$6.99
00697416	Book/Online Audio	$14.99

EASY POP CHRISTMAS RHYTHMS
00278177	Book	$6.99
00278175	Book/Online Audio	$14.99

LEAD LICKS
00697345	Book/Online Audio	$10.99

RHYTHM RIFFS
00697346	Book/Online Audio	$10.99

STYLISTIC METHODS

ACOUSTIC GUITAR
00697347	Book/Online Audio	$16.99
00237969	Acoustic Guitar Songs (with Online Audio)	$16.99

BLUEGRASS GUITAR
00697405	Book/Online Audio	$16.99

BLUES GUITAR
00697326	Book/Online Audio	$16.99
00697385	Blues Guitar Songs (with Online Audio)	$14.99

BRAZILIAN GUITAR
00697415	Book/Online Audio	$14.99

CHRISTIAN GUITAR
00695947	Book/Online Audio	$12.99
00697408	Christian Guitar Songs	$14.99

CLASSICAL GUITAR
00697376	Book/Online Audio	$15.99
00697388	Classical Guitar Pieces	$9.99

COUNTRY GUITAR
00697337	Book/Online Audio	$22.99
00697400	Country Guitar Songs	$16.99

FINGERSTYLE GUITAR
00697378	Book/Online Audio	$19.99
00697432	Fingerstyle Guitar Songs (with Online Audio)	$14.99

FLAMENCO GUITAR
00697363	Book/Online Audio	$15.99

FOLK GUITAR
00697414	Book/Online Audio	$14.99

JAZZ GUITAR
00695359	Book/Online Audio	$19.99
00697386	Jazz Guitar Songs	$14.95

JAZZ-ROCK FUSION
00697387	Book/Online Audio	$19[...]

ROCK GUITAR
00697319	Book/Online Audio	$1[...]
00697383	Rock Guitar Songs	$1[...]

ROCKABILLY GUITAR
00697407	Book/Online Audio	$1[...]

R&B GUITAR
00697356	Book/CD Pack	$1[...]
00697433	R&B Guitar Songs	$14[...]

TENOR GUITAR
00148330	Book/Online Audio	$12[...]

REFERENCE

ARPEGGIO FINDER
00697351	9" x 12" Edition	$8[...]

INCREDIBLE CHORD FINDER
00697200	6" x 9" Edition	$8[...]
00697208	9" x 12" Edition	$8[...]

INCREDIBLE SCALE FINDER
00695568	6" x 9" Edition	$8[...]
00695490	9" x 12" Edition	$8[...]

GUITAR CHORD, SCALE & ARPEGGIO FINDE[...]
00697410		$19[...]

GUITAR SETUP & MAINTENANCE
00697427	6" x 9" Edition	$14[...]
00697421	9" x 12" Edition	$12[...]

GUITAR TECHNIQUES
00697389	Book/CD Pack	$14[...]

GUITAR PRACTICE PLANNER
00697401		$5[...]

MUSIC THEORY FOR GUITARISTS
00695790	Book/Online Audio	$19[...]

HAL•LEONARD®

www.halleonard.com

Prices, contents and availability subject to change without notice.